Economics
New Ways of Thinking

Applying the Principles Workbook

Scott Wolla

Hibbing High School, Hibbing, Minnesota

EMC
Publishing

St. Paul, Minnesota

Developmental Editors: Cheryl Drivdahl, Barbara Sheridan
Assistant Editor: Ashley Kuehl
Proofreaders: Laura Nelson, Erin Saladin

Electronic Design and Production Manager: Shelley Clubb
Cover Designer: Leslie Anderson
Interior Designer: Matthias Frasch
Production Specialist: Jack Ross

ISBN 978-0-8219-3404-3

© 2007 by EMC Publishing, LLC
875 Montreal Way
St. Paul, MN 55102
E-mail: educate@emcp.com
Web site: www.emcp.com

Printed in the United States of America

16 15 14 13 12 11 10   XXX   7 8 9 10

CONTENTS

UNIT IV Macroeconomics

Unit V Trade and Investment

PREFACE

A good curriculum uses an excellent textbook as a foundation and a springboard for further learning. I have had the opportunity to read many textbooks in my teaching career, and I have found *Economics: New Ways of Thinking* superior in presenting complex economics issues in a clear, precise way that is accessible to high school students. It goes beyond a simple listing of terms and concepts, and moves to something that is readable and engaging. It was to my benefit that I started with such a wonderful textbook in the writing of this workbook.

The study of economics is at its best when students are active participants. It was from that belief that I wrote this *Applying the Principles Workbook.* In creating this book, I attempted to give students a bit of the actual experience of economics and to tie that experience to the textbook as closely as possible. The lessons attempt to push students beyond the stage of vocabulary retention to a level at which they are interacting with the content. In areas where the workbook stretches beyond the scope of the textbook, great care was taken to provide the necessary definitions and direction, while maintaining a direct connection with the textbook. I hope the result helps you provide an atmosphere of economic literacy in your classroom.

Scott Wolla

About the Author

Scott Wolla teaches economics at Hibbing High School, in Hibbing, Minnesota. He received his bachelor of science degree from Minnesota State University Moorhead and his master's degree from Bemidji State University, Minnesota.

Scott was named Teacher of the Year by the Minnesota Council for the Social Studies in 2006, and Innovative Economic Educator of the Year by the Minnesota Council on Economic Education in 2003. He was a nominee for Minnesota Teacher of the Year in 2006 and a finalist for the National Council on Economic Education's NASDAQ National Teaching Award in 2005. Scott is also the coach of an award-winning Economics Challenge team.

Acknowledgments

I would like to thank Bob Cassel, of EMC Publishing, for offering me the opportunity to write this workbook; Roger A. Arnold, author of the student textbook, for reviewing the workbook material and ensuring that it aligns with the textbook content; and Barbara Sheridan for her careful and complete edit of the workbook activities.

Dedication

To my wife, Dawn, for her support and encouragement.

Name: _____ Date: _____

CHAPTER 1, SECTION 1

Scarcity

Guns or Butter

Economists often speak of the way a society allocates its resources between military and consumer spending as a method for choosing guns or butter. Of course, guns represent resources allocated to a nation's defense; butter represents resources allocated for consumer goods. Economists use the phrase "guns *or* butter" because scarcity mandates that we choose how to use available resources.

Illustrate the relationship between guns and butter as directed in question 1.

1. Use the following data to draw a production possibilities frontier (PPF) on the grid shown.

Guns	Butter
0	15
3	14
8	11
11	7
12	4
13	0

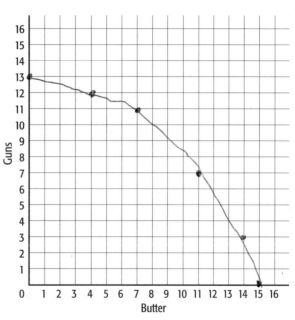

An Economy's Production Possibilities Frontier for Guns and Butter

Use the graph you created in question 1 to answer questions 2–8.

2. Can this economy produce 6 units of guns and 12 units of butter? Explain.

   yes, it is within the PPF arc

   _____

3. Can this economy produce 11 units of guns and 11 units of butter? Explain.

   No, it is outside the PPF arc

   _____

4. What does this PPF represent?

_____

_____

5. How does this PPF illustrate the concept of scarcity?

_____

_____

6. How does this PPF illustrate the concept of opportunity cost?

_____

_____

_____

7. If the economy is presently producing 0 units of guns and 15 units of butter, what is the opportunity cost of increasing the production of guns from 0 units to 3 units?

_____

8. If the economy is presently producing 12 units of guns and 4 units of butter, what is the opportunity cost of increasing the production of butter from 4 units to 11 units?

_____

_____

The Production Possibilities Frontier and Efficiency

The PPF represents what an economy can produce when it is using all its resources efficiently. As long as the economy is producing at a point on its PPF, it is producing at an **efficient** level and using all its resources.

When an economy is already using all its resources efficiently, it cannot use the same resources to produce something beyond, or outside, its PPF. Therefore, economists say that a point outside an economy's PPF is **unattainable.**

An economy _can_ produce at a point inside its PPF. However, if an economy is producing at a point inside its PPF, then either the economy is not using all its resources or it is using them inefficiently. Economists label a point inside the PPF **underutilization** because such a point indicates that the economy is underutilizing its resources.

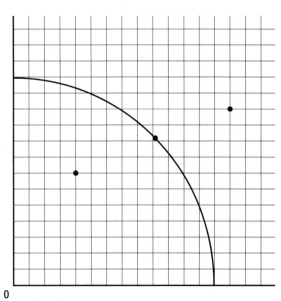

The PPF and Efficiency

Efficiency, unattainability, and underutilization are shown on the PPF and Efficiency graph on the previous page. Use the graph to answer questions 9–11.

9. The point that represents an unattainable point is _____.

10. The point that represents underutilization is _____.

11. An economy that is using all its resources efficiently is producing at point _____.

Shifts in the Production Possibilities Frontier

The location of the PPF for an economy is determined mostly by the amount of resources available and the level of technology in the society. If more resources become available or the level of technology increases, more goods and services can be produced and the PPF will shift to the right. If the amount of resources diminishes, the economy can no longer produce at previous levels and the PPF will shift to the left.

Write your answers to questions 12 and 13 on the lines provided.

12. What two things would cause the PPF of an economy to shift to the right (outward)?

_____

_____

13. What would cause the PPF of an economy to shift to the left (inward)?

_____

_____

Use the Shifts in the PPF graph to answer questions 14–19. Assume that the PPF begins at the location labeled C. Read question 14 and determine the direction (left or right) that the PPF will move from location C in response to the event described. Then write the letter of the new location. Now read question 15 and determine the direction the PPF will move from the location you decided on in question 14. Then write the letter of the new location. Continue to determine the direction and location for each subsequent event.

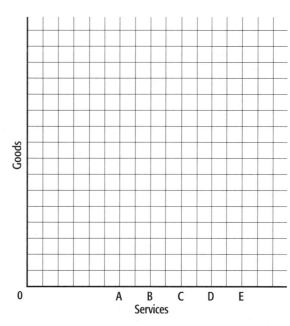

Shifts in the PPF

14. The invention of the lightbulb allows laborers to work later hours and introduces the midnight shift.

Direction: _____ *Location:* _____

15. A major drought makes much of America's farmland unproductive.

Direction: _____ *Location:* _____

16. The baby boomer generation starts to retire, and millions leave the workforce.

Direction: _____ *Location:* _____

17. The invention of the Internet allows people to communicate, do research, and conduct business from remote locations.

Direction: _____ *Location:* _____

18. The U.S. government loosens immigration requirements, allowing millions of skilled workers to enter the country.

Direction: _____ *Location:* _____

19. The invention of the cell phone allows people to communicate while commuting or from remote locations.

Direction: _____ *Location:* _____

A society makes choices that determine how it will allocate its resources between guns and butter. For each of the events in questions 20–23, circle either *guns* or *butter* to indicate whether the event would cause a shift along the PPF toward producing more guns or toward producing more butter.

20. After World War I, America pursues a policy of "return to normalcy" and defense spending is cut.

Shift toward guns or butter.

21. America enters World War II.

Shift toward guns or butter.

22. The Cold War escalates and the number of nuclear warheads increases.

Shift toward guns or butter.

23. After the prosperous 1990s, the terrorist attacks of September 11, 2001, lead the United States into wars in Afghanistan and Iraq and to increased spending on homeland security.

Shift toward guns or butter.

For question 24, circle the letter of the correct answer.

24. Some economists argue that unemployment is the main issue that should concern government officials, because unemployment represents underutilized resources. Which of the following situations best describes this view of unemployment?

    a. a point inside the PPF

    b. a point outside the PPF

    c. a shift of the PPF to the right

    d. a shift of the PPF to the left

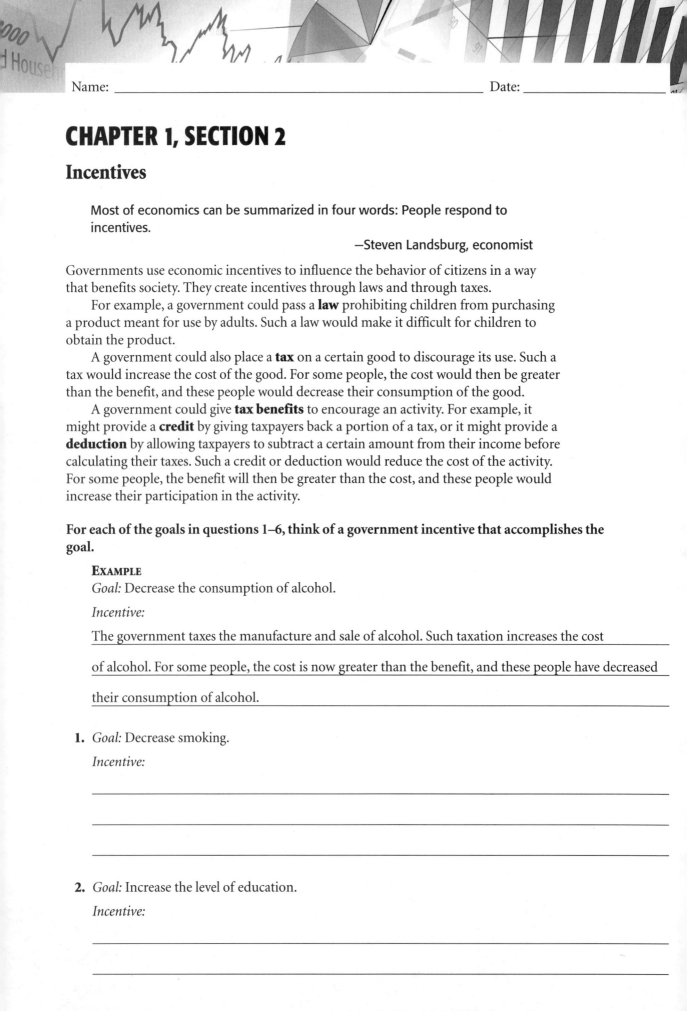

Name: _____ Date: _____

CHAPTER 1, SECTION 2

Incentives

> Most of economics can be summarized in four words: People respond to incentives.
>
> —Steven Landsburg, economist

Governments use economic incentives to influence the behavior of citizens in a way that benefits society. They create incentives through laws and through taxes.

For example, a government could pass a **law** prohibiting children from purchasing a product meant for use by adults. Such a law would make it difficult for children to obtain the product.

A government could also place a **tax** on a certain good to discourage its use. Such a tax would increase the cost of the good. For some people, the cost would then be greater than the benefit, and these people would decrease their consumption of the good.

A government could give **tax benefits** to encourage an activity. For example, it might provide a **credit** by giving taxpayers back a portion of a tax, or it might provide a **deduction** by allowing taxpayers to subtract a certain amount from their income before calculating their taxes. Such a credit or deduction would reduce the cost of the activity. For some people, the benefit will then be greater than the cost, and these people would increase their participation in the activity.

For each of the goals in questions 1–6, think of a government incentive that accomplishes the goal.

EXAMPLE

Goal: Decrease the consumption of alcohol.

Incentive:

The government taxes the manufacture and sale of alcohol. Such taxation increases the cost

of alcohol. For some people, the cost is now greater than the benefit, and these people have decreased

their consumption of alcohol.

1. *Goal:* Decrease smoking.

   Incentive:

   _____

   _____

   _____

2. *Goal:* Increase the level of education.

   Incentive:

   _____

   _____

3. *Goal:* Increase the rate of private home ownership.

Incentive:

_____

_____

_____

4. *Goal:* Decrease the consumption of fuel oil.

Incentive:

_____

_____

_____

5. *Goal:* Increase the rate of personal savings.

Incentive:

_____

_____

6. *Goal:* Increase donations to charities.

Incentive:

_____

_____

For questions 7 and 8, write two goals (other than those mentioned in questions 1–6) that you think would benefit society, and describe an incentive that will accomplish each goal.

7. *Goal:*

_____

_____

Incentive:

_____

_____

8. *Goal:*

_____

_____

Incentive:

_____

_____

Refer to the goals and incentives in questions 1–6 as you answer questions 9 and 10.

9. What is the trade-off of using tax benefits as incentives?

_____

_____

10. Could any of these incentives have unintended effects? Explain.

_____

_____

_____

Economists assume that people are rational beings who weigh the costs and benefits of various options before making a decision. In short, they view human behavior as a response to incentives.

Suppose absenteeism is a problem in your school. In questions 11–17, your task is to analyze the present costs and benefits of attending school, come up with an incentive system that will improve attendance at your school, and analyze that system.

11. What are the present costs?

Costs of attending school:

_____

Costs of skipping school:

_____

12. What are the present benefits?

Benefits of attending school:

_____

Benefits of skipping school:

_____

13. In creating your incentive plan, use one or more of these options: (1) decrease the costs of attending school, (2) increase the costs of skipping school, (3) increase the benefits of attending school, and (4) decrease the benefits of skipping school. Write your incentive plan below.

_____

_____

_____

_____

_____

_____

_____

_____

14. How will your incentive plan increase student attendance?

_____

_____

_____

15. Is your plan practical and feasible? Explain.

_____

_____

_____

16. What are the trade-offs to using these incentives?

_____

_____

_____

17. Could any of these incentives have unintended effects? Explain.

_____

_____

_____

CHAPTER 1, SECTION 3

Resources

Use the following key to label each of the resources in questions 1–16 as land, labor, capital, or entrepreneurship. If a resource is land, identify it as either renewable or nonrenewable. If a resource is a capital good, identify it as either physical or human. (*Hint:* Physical capital is a tangible, human-made resource—such as tools or machinery—used to produce other goods and services. Human capital is the knowledge and skills a worker gains through education and experience.)

Ld-r = land (renewable)
Ld-n = land (nonrenewable)
Lbr = labor
C-p = capital (physical)
C-h = capital (human)
E = entrepreneurship

1. coal _____Ld-n_____

2. telephone _____C-p_____

3. natural gas _____Ld-r_____

4. computer _____C-p_____

5. truck driver _____Lbr_____

6. accountant _____Lbr_____

7. forklift _____C-p_____

8. oak trees _____Ld-r_____

9. corn _____Ld-r_____

10. education _____C-h_____

11. Bill Gates _____E_____

12. cotton _____Ld-r_____

13. gold _____Ld-n_____

14. hammer _____C-p_____

15. Henry Ford _____E_____

16. lawyer _____Lbr_____

Look at your desk at school or at home. For each of the categories identified in questions 17–20, determine the resources that were used to produce the desk.

17. land

_____

18. labor

_____

19. capital

_____

_____

Applying the Principles Workbook

20. entrepreneurship

_____

_____

Write your answer to question 21 on the lines provided.

21. As a student at school, which of the four economic resources are you? Defend your answer.

_____

_____

_____

_____

CHAPTER 2, SECTION 1

Economic Systems

1-14

Three Economic Questions

In questions 1–3, state the three economic questions that all nations must answer, and summarize what each question means.

1. *Economic question:*

   What goods will be produced?

   Summary of economic question:

   We have to choose which good will be produced in higher quantities

2. *Economic question:*

   How will the goods be produced?

   Summary of economic question:

   How will the good be made (method) and who will control whats made

3. *Economic question:*

   For whom will the goods be produced?

   Summary of economic question:

   Who will be willing to pay for the goods

Comparing Free Enterprise and Socialism

Write your answers to questions 4–7 on the lines provided.

4. What is free enterprise?

   An economic system which individuals own most, if not all, of the resources and control their use

5. What two terms are sometimes used to refer to free enterprise?

Capitalism and market economy

6. What is socialism?

Where government controls and may own many of the resources

7. What two terms are confused with *socialism* but actually refer to types of socialism?

Communism and command economy

Answer question 8 by completing the table provided.

8. Comparing information is often easier when the information is organized in a table. Complete the following table to compare free enterprise and socialism in six major areas.

Area	Free enterprise	Socialism
Resources		
Government's role in the economy		
Economic plans		
Income distribution		
Controlling prices		
Private property		

Mixed and Traditional Economies

Write your answers to questions 9–12 on the lines provided.

9. What is a mixed economy?

_____

_____

_____

10. Why is a mixed economy not considered a major economic system along with free enterprise and socialism?

_____

_____

_____

11. What is a traditional economy?

_____

_____

_____

12. Why is a traditional economy not considered a major economic system?

_____

_____

_____

The United States' Mixed Economy

The U.S. economy, which is a mixed economy, includes elements of both free enterprise and socialism. Write your answers to questions 13 and 14 on the lines provided.

13. What elements of free enterprise does the U.S. economy include?

_____

_____

14. What elements of socialism does the U.S. economy include?

_____

_____

1-18

CHAPTER 2, SECTION 1

The Visions

Answer question 1 by completing the table.

1. Complete the following table by identifying some of the differences between Adam Smith and Karl Marx.

Topic	Adam Smith	Karl Marx
Place and year of birth		
Education		
Major work		
Vision		

In questions 2–5, briefly describe the views of Adam Smith on the topics listed.

2. self-interest

_____

_____

3. division of labor

_____

_____

4. competition

_____

_____

5. government

_____

_____

In questions 6–8, briefly describe the views of Karl Marx on the topics listed.

6. value of produced goods

_____

_____

7. capitalists

_____

_____

8. development of nations

_____

_____

Use the following key to label each of the statements in questions 9–18 as more like the free enterprise vision of Adam Smith or as more like the socialist vision of Karl Marx.

S = Adam Smith, free enterprise vision
M = Karl Marx, socialist vision

9. _____ Resources are owned by private individuals.

10. _____ Government decision makers write economic plans.

11. _____ Private property is sacred.

12. _____ Government makes major decisions concerning the use of resources and the production of goods.

13. _____ Much attention is given to distribute income away from high earners toward low earners.

14. _____ Government owns and controls many resources.

15. _____ Government does not attempt to control prices.

16. _____ Government plays a small role in the economy.

17. _____ Government sets wages and the prices of goods.

18. _____ Government owns most property and uses it for the benefit of the people.

CHAPTER 2, SECTION 2

Globalization

Evidence of the Movement Toward Globalization

Certain facts provide evidence that globalization is happening. In questions 1–6, describe how the facts listed indicate the trend toward globalization.

1. decline in U.S. tariff rates

_____

_____

2. increase in foreign exchange trading

_____

_____

3. increase in foreign direct investment

_____

_____

4. increase in U.S. personal foreign investment

_____

_____

5. increase in membership in the World Trade Organization (WTO)

_____

_____

6. easier worldwide communication

_____

_____

_____

Causes of the Movement Toward Globalization

In questions 7–9, explain how each of the factors listed has led to the recent period of globalization.

7. the end of the Cold War

_____

_____

_____

8. advancing technology

_____

_____

_____

9. policy changes

_____

_____

_____

Benefits of Globalization

In questions 10 and 11, list the major benefits put forth by those who favor globalization. Then describe how each is a good thing. Write your answers on the lines provided.

10. *Benefit:*

_____

Description:

_____

_____

_____

11. *Benefit:*

_____

Description:

_____

_____

_____

_____

Costs of Globalization

In questions 12–14, list and describe the major costs put forth by the critics of globalization. Then summarize the response that supporters of globalization might offer for each cost. Write your answers on the lines provided.

12. *Cost:*

_____

Description:

_____

_____

_____

Response:

_____

_____

_____

13. *Cost:*

_____

Description:

_____

_____

_____

Response:

_____

_____

_____

14. *Cost:*

_____

Description:

_____

_____

_____

Response:

_____

_____

_____

Debating Globalization

Write your answers to questions 15 and 16 on the lines provided.

15. Do you think Adam Smith or Karl Marx would be more supportive of globalization? Explain.

_____

_____

_____

16. Examine the arguments of the critics and the supporters of globalization. Do you agree with the critics or the supporters? Would you like to see more or less globalization in the future? How will globalization affect you personally? How will globalization affect your local economy? Write a letter to the editor of the *Wall Street Journal* or to your local paper, expressing your ideas and arguments about globalization.

_____

_____

_____

_____

_____

_____

_____

_____

_____

_____

_____

_____

_____

Name: ______________________________ Date: ______________

CHAPTER 3, SECTION 1

Characteristics of Free Enterprise

Three Economic Questions

In questions 1–3, explain how free enterprise answers the three economic questions all nations must decide how to answer.

1. What goods will be produced?

____

____

2. How will the goods be produced?

____

____

3. For whom will the goods be produced?

____

____

Circular Flow

The following diagram shows the economic relationships that exist between different economic groups in the U.S. economy. Use the diagram to answer questions 4–9.

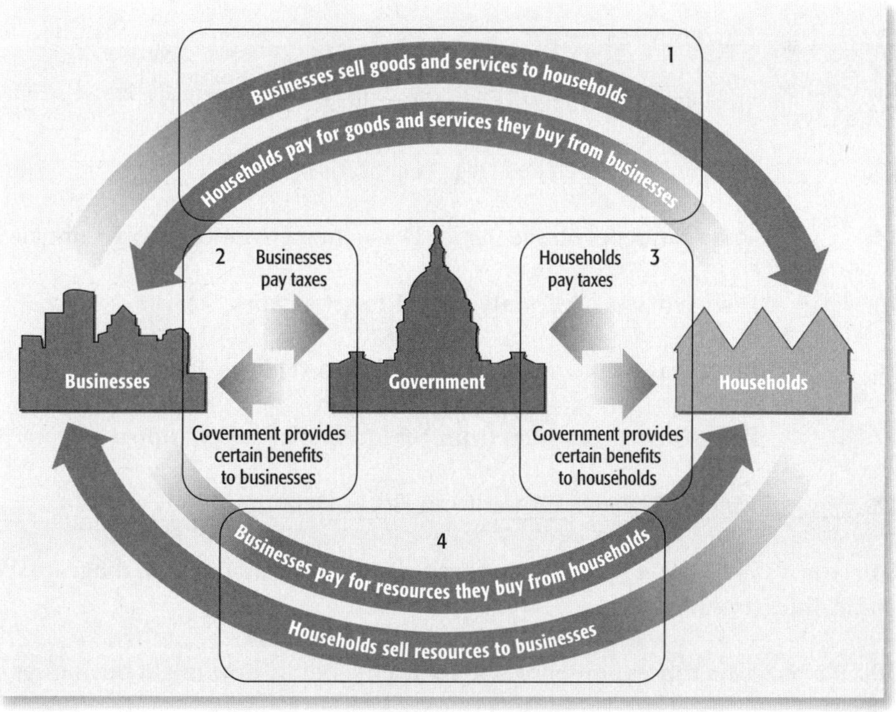

The Circular Flow of Economic Activity in the U.S. Economy

4. What economic activities flow from businesses to households?

_____

_____

5. What economic activities flow from households to businesses?

_____

_____

6. What economic activities flow from government to households?

_____

7. What economic activities flow from households to government?

_____

8. What economic activities flow from government to businesses?

_____

9. What economic activities flow from businesses to government?

_____

In questions 10–18, identify the part of the circular flow diagram in which the economic activity listed occurs. Write 1, 2, 3, or 4 in the blanks provided.

10. _____ Mycah attends a public school.

11. _____ Travis buys a new car.

12. _____ Mikayla works 20 hours a week at Burger Barn.

13. _____ Trish does research at a large corporation.

14. _____ Microsoft relies on the Justice Department to enforce copyright laws.

15. _____ Dianne drives on County Road 1 to get to work.

16. _____ Bruce leases his commercial building to Widgets, Inc.

17. _____ Dawn buys a computer from her local office supply store.

18. _____ Vanh buys a lawn mower from Home Depot.

Questions 19–21 relate to the flow of resources in the circular flow diagram. Write your answers on the lines provided.

19. If a recession causes households to reduce spending, how might businesses be affected?

_____

_____

20. If government raises taxes on businesses, how might households be affected?

_____

21. If government cuts taxes on households, how might businesses be affected?

_____

Features

In questions 22–26, list the major features or characteristics that define free enterprise. Then explain what each feature means to people in a free enterprise system. Write your answers in the blanks provided.

22. *Feature:*

_____

Explanation:

_____

_____

_____

23. *Feature:*

_____

Explanation:

_____

_____

_____

24. *Feature:*

_____

Explanation:

_____

_____

_____

25. *Feature:*

_____

Explanation:

_____

_____

_____

26. *Feature:*

_____

Explanation:

_____

_____

_____

Write your answers to questions 27 and 28 in the spaces provided.

27. How would the operation of free enterprise be affected if any of its characteristics were hindered?

_____

_____

28. Explain the role of economic incentives in your life. What economic incentives do you react to every day? For example, what economic incentives motivate you to go to school and to drive the speed limit?

_____

_____

_____

CHAPTER 3, SECTION 2

Profit and Loss in Free Enterprise

Complete the formulas in questions 1–4.

1. Total revenue = _____.

2. Total cost = _____.

3. Profit = _____.

4. Loss = _____.

Bryan sells gadgets at a price of $7 apiece. His average cost is $5 per gadget. On Monday, Bryan sold 10 gadgets; on Tuesday, he sold 7 gadgets; on Wednesday, he sold 9 gadgets; on Thursday, he sold 11 gadgets; and on Friday, he sold 13 gadgets.

Write your answers to questions 5–8 in the blanks provided.

5. What was Bryan's total revenue for the week? _____

6. What was Bryan's total cost for the week? _____

7. Did Bryan have a profit or a loss for the week? _____

8. What was the dollar amount of Bryan's profit or loss for the week? _____

Write your answers to questions 9 and 10 in the blanks provided.

9. You have likely heard someone say, "Every time I turn on the television, all I see are reality shows, and every time I turn on the radio, all I hear is hip-hop music. Why do television networks and radio stations all broadcast the same content? Why can't they be original for a change?" What could you say about profit and loss as signals to someone who says this?

   _____

   _____

   _____

   _____

   _____

   _____

10. Today, companies like Toyota and Honda are earning large profits from the manufacture and sale of hybrid cars. What do economists predict will be the response of other auto manufacturers?

_____

_____

_____

_____

_____

_____

CHAPTER 3, SECTION 3

The Ethics of Free Enterprise

An Ethical System

Just as ethics—the principles of conduct, such as right and wrong, morality and immorality, good and bad—applies to the behavior of individuals, ethics applies to the behavior of an economic system. In questions 1–4, list and describe the goals that free enterprise needs to meet in order to be considered an ethical economic system.

1. *Goal:*

_____

Description:

_____

_____

2. *Goal:*

_____

Description:

_____

_____

3. *Goal:*

_____

Description:

_____

_____

4. *Goal:*

_____

Description:

_____

Government Subsidies

One role of government is to keep the country's economic system running smoothly. If most citizens have jobs, people are generally happier with government's role. In some cases, the government might subsidize failing or struggling businesses in order to save jobs. Write your answers to questions 5 and 6 in the blanks provided.

5. What might be the reason why a business is failing?

_____

_____

_____

_____

6. Why might people consider it to be unethical to save a failing business?

_____

_____

_____

_____

Key Documents

In questions 7–9, identify the feature of free enterprise contained in the document listed. Then describe the document's reference to the feature. Write your answers in the blanks provided.

7. Bill of Rights

   Feature:

   _____

   Description:

   _____

   _____

8. Declaration of Independence

   Feature:

   _____

   Description:

   _____

   _____

9. U.S. Constitution

Feature:

_____

Description:

_____

_____

Rights and Responsibilities

Write your answer to question 10 on the lines provided.

10. People in a free enterprise economy have certain rights, but they also have responsibilities. What are people's responsibilities in a free enterprise economy?

_____

_____

_____

_____

CHAPTER 3, SECTION 4

Entrepreneurs

Write your answers to questions 1–4 in the blanks provided.

1. How does the following quotation relate to the success of some entrepreneurs?

    Necessity is the mother of invention.
    —Plato

    _____

    _____

    _____

    _____

    _____

    _____

2. Some economists say that entrepreneurship is something that cannot be taught but, instead, is a natural talent that some people have. Do you agree? Why or why not?

    _____

    _____

    _____

    _____

    _____

3. Bill Gates, Steven Jobs, and Ted Turner are entrepreneurs whose work has made them among the wealthiest people in the world. Why is it necessary to allow entrepreneurs to benefit from their work?

    _____

    _____

    _____

    _____

    _____

4. How do we all benefit from the work of entrepreneurs?

_____

_____

_____

_____

_____

_____

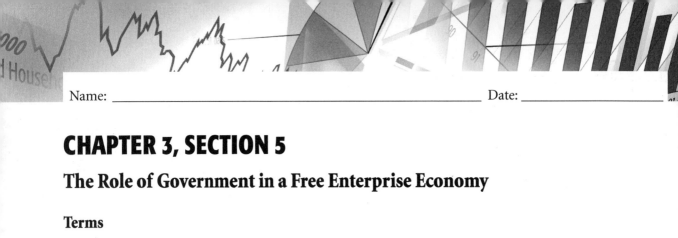

Name: _____ Date: _____

CHAPTER 3, SECTION 5

The Role of Government in a Free Enterprise Economy

Terms

Fill in the blanks in questions 1–7 to be sure you understand some important economic terms.

1. One person's consumption of a(n) _____ takes away from another person's consumption.

2. Individuals can be excluded (physically prohibited) from consuming a(n) _____ or a(n) _____.

3. Individuals cannot be excluded (physically prohibited) from consuming a(n) _____.

4. In a free enterprise economy, firms will not produce _____ because people will not pay for them.

5. A(n) _____ receives the benefits of a good without paying for it.

6. A positive externality is a(n) _____ of an action that is felt by others.

7. A negative externality is a(n) _____ of an act that is felt by others.

Types of Goods

Use the following key to label each of the goods in questions 8–15 as a private good, an excludable public good, or a nonexcludable public good.

> P = private good
> E = excludable public good
> N = nonexcludable public good

8. _____ fireworks display

9. _____ public radio

10. _____ mp3 player

11. _____ dam

12. _____ toll road

13. _____ national defense

14. _____ rock concert

15. _____ hamburger

Applying the Principles Workbook © EMC Publishing

Externalities

Use the following key to label each of the situations described in questions 16–23 as a positive externality or a negative externality. Then explain why the externality is positive or negative.

P = positive externality
N = negative externality

16. _____ Your neighbor has loud parties late into the night, keeping you awake.

_____

_____

17. _____ Your neighbor has a large oak tree that shades your yard.

_____

_____

18. _____ Your neighbor does not take care of his house; the house is literally falling apart.

_____

_____

19. _____ Your community has excellent schools.

_____

_____

20. _____ The person sitting next to you in a restaurant is talking loudly on a cell phone.

_____

_____

21. _____ A factory in your town spews pollution into the air.

_____

_____

22. _____ Your state requires children to get vaccinated for common diseases.

_____

_____

23. _____ People in your community shoplift at local stores.

_____

_____

Write your answers to questions 24 and 25 in the blanks provided.

24. How can government encourage the production of positive externalities?

_____

_____

25. How can government discourage the production of negative externalities?

_____

_____

A negative externality places some costs on third parties. A negative externality is **internalized** if the party that generates the negative externality is made to feel the costs of the negative externality. To illustrate, suppose Johnson smokes cigarettes and imposes a negative externality on Smith. Let's go further and say this negative externality is equal to a cost of $2 (as far as Smith is concerned). If Johnson can be made to feel this $2 cost, then the negative externality has been internalized.

You might want to think of internalizing a negative externality the same way you think of a boomerang. When you throw a boomerang outward from you, it returns to you (assuming it was thrown correctly). Johnson "throws" the smoke outward from his cigarette, and while the smoke does not return to him, the cost of the smoke to a third party does revert to him.

With this as background, assume you live in a large city where most people use cars as their means of transportation. As the city has grown, air pollution problems have worsened from the additional cars on the crowded highways. Some people complain to the city council about respiratory problems caused by the pollution.

In response, the city council is considering various solutions to the pollution problem. Members of the council have proposed the following three solutions.

Proposal 1: The solution is to add highway lanes. The money for highway lane construction would come from an increase in the general sales tax.

Proposal 2: The solution is to build a railroad commuter line. The revenue to build the railroad commuter line would come from an increase in the general sales tax.

Proposal 3: The solution is to impose a tax on drivers for driving.

Use the information above and your knowledge of externalities to analyze the problem and the proposals. Write your answers to questions 26–31 in the blanks provided.

26. What negative externality exists here?

_____

_____

27. Will the negative externality be reduced or eliminated by proposal 1? Explain.

_____

_____

_____

28. Will the negative externality be internalized by proposal 1? Explain.

_____

_____

_____

29. Will the negative externality be reduced or eliminated by proposal 2? Explain.

_____

_____

_____

30. Will the negative externality be internalized by proposal 2? Explain.

_____

_____

_____

31. Will the negative externality be internalized by proposal 3? Explain.

_____

_____

_____

_____

Name: _____ Date: _____

CHAPTER 4, SECTION 1
Demand!

Demand and the Law of Demand

To be sure you understand demand and the law of demand, fill in the blanks in questions 1–4.

1. The two conditions of demand are _____ and

   _____.

2. The law of demand says that as the price of a good increases, the quantity demanded of the good

   _____.

3. The law of demand says that as the price of a good decreases, the quantity demanded of the good

   _____.

4. According to the law of demand, price and quantity demanded move in _____
   direction(s).

Demand Schedules and Demand Curves

The law of demand can be represented in numbers using a **demand schedule** or it can
be represented as a graph showing a **demand curve**.

Answer question 5 to illustrate the connection between a demand schedule and a demand curve.

5. Use the demand schedule below to create a
   demand curve for Simon's consumption of
   music downloads on the grid shown. Label the
   curve D_1.

DEMAND SCHEDULE FOR SIMON

Price (dollars)	Quantity demanded (units)
$7	1
$6	2
$5	3
$4	4
$3	5
$2	6
$1	7

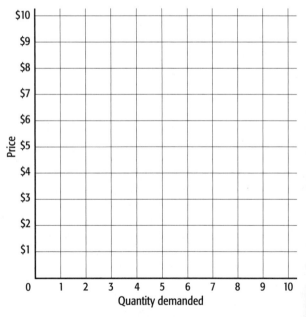

Demand Curve Derived from Demand Schedule

Applying the Principles Workbook
© EMC Publishing

Use the graph you created in question 5 to answer questions 6–10.

6. The demand curve shows that at a price of $7, Simon will buy _____ music download(s), and at a price of $1, he will buy _____ music download(s).

7. Simon's buying behavior demonstrates the law of _____.

8. Simon's change in buying behavior at different prices is a change in _____.

9. Simon is not willing to pay $7 for every download because his utility (satisfaction) decreases as he downloads more and more music. Economists call this concept the

   _____.

10. How does the concept in question 9 explain the slope of the demand curve?

   _____

   _____

   _____

All people do not have the same demand for a good. Some people have a greater willingness and ability to purchase a good than other people do.

Use the information in question 11 to compare the demand curves of two different people for the same good.

11. Use the demand schedule below to create a demand curve for Carla's consumption of music downloads. Draw the graph on the grid in question 5. Label the curve D_2.

DEMAND SCHEDULE FOR CARLA

Price (dollars)	Quantity demanded (units)
$7	4
$6	5
$5	6
$4	7
$3	8
$2	9
$1	10

To answer questions 12–16, use the graph in question 5, which now shows both Simon's and Carla's demand curves.

12. Carla's demand curve (D_2) is to the _____ of Simon's demand curve (D_1).

13. For each of the listed prices, Carla is willing and able to buy _____ music downloads than Simon is willing and able to buy.

14. At each of the possible quantities, Carla is willing and able to pay a _____ price than Simon is willing and able to pay.

15. The demand curves you created on the grid in question 5 are _____ demand curves.

16. Suppose Simon and Carla are the only buyers of music downloads. How would you create a market demand curve from the demand curves you drew on the grid in question 5?

_____

_____

_____

CHAPTER 4, SECTION 2
The Demand Curve Shifts

Changes in Demand and Shifts in Demand Curves

When demand changes, the demand curve shifts. Fill in the blanks in questions 1 and 2 with the correct answers.

1. If demand increases, the demand curve shifts _____right_____, meaning that buyers want to buy _____more_____ of a good at each and every price.

2. If demand decreases, the demand curve shifts _____left_____, meaning that buyers want to buy _____less_____ of a good at each and every price.

Factors That Cause Shifts in Demand Curves

In questions 3–7, list five factors that cause demand curves to shift. For each factor, describe how the factor affects the demand for a good (whether the factor causes demand to rise or fall).

3. *Factor:*

   Income

   Description:

   It depends what type of good it is, but the demand will change based on whether the good is normal, inferior, or neutral

4. *Factor:*

   Preferences

   Description:

   If people favor things more it shifts right and if they don't favor it shifts left

5. *Factor:*

   Prices of Related goods

   Description:

   Substitutes: as the price of one goes up, then the demand for the substitute goes up. Complements: as the price of one goes up, then the demand for the other goes down

6. *Factor:*

Number of Buyers

Description:

The more buyers, the higher the demand. Vice versa

7. *Factor:*

Future Price

Description:

If price is expected to rise in the future, then demand is high now. If price is expected to drop in the future, then demand is low now.

Demand Versus Quantity Demanded

Demand is not the same as quantity demanded. Answer questions 8–11 on the lines provided.

8. What will cause a change in the demand for a good?

_____

_____

9. What will cause a change in the quantity demanded of a good?

_____

_____

10. How is a change in demand represented on a graph?

_____

_____

11. How is a change in quantity demanded represented on a graph?

_____

_____

Changes in Demand and in Quantity Demanded

In questions 12–17, fill in the blanks to describe how each event will affect the demand for large sport utility vehicles (SUVs).

12. The price of gasoline hits $3 per gallon.

Will the demand for large SUVs increase, decrease, or stay the same?

_____

In which direction will the demand curve shift?

_____

Which of the five factors causes the shift?

_____

13. Smaller, sportier "crossover vehicles" hit the market and become the latest craze.
Will the demand for large SUVs increase, decrease, or stay the same?

_____

In which direction will the demand curve shift?

_____

Which of the five factors causes the shift?

_____

14. Rising steel prices cause the prices of SUVs to rise.
Will the demand for large SUVs increase, decrease, or stay the same?

_____

In which direction will the demand curve shift?

_____

Which of the five factors causes the shift?

_____

15. Government data show that the incomes of Americans are expected to rise faster than ever over the next year.
Will the demand for large SUVs increase, decrease, or stay the same?

_____

In which direction will the demand curve shift?

_____

Which of the five factors causes the shift?

_____

16. Word leaks to consumers that General Motors and Ford plan to offer big rebates on SUVs next month.
Will the demand for large SUVs increase, decrease, or stay the same?

_____

In which direction will the demand curve shift?

_____

Which of the five factors causes the shift?

_____

17. The government loosens immigration laws, allowing millions of immigrants into the country. Will the demand for large SUVs increase, decrease, or stay the same?

_____

In which direction will the demand curve shift?

_____

Which of the five factors causes the shift?

_____

The Relationship Between Income and Demand

As a result of an increase in wages from his employer, Kramer increased his consumption of Junior Mints and Bosco chocolate-flavored syrup, decreased his consumption of fried chicken, and maintained the same consumption of yogurt.

In questions 18–21, identify each of the goods consumed by Kramer as a normal good, an inferior good, or a neutral good.

18. Junior Mints _____

19. Bosco chocolate-flavored syrup _____

20. fried chicken _____

21. yogurt _____

In questions 22–25, identify which one of graphs (a), (b), and (c) illustrates the change to Kramer's demand curve for each of the goods.

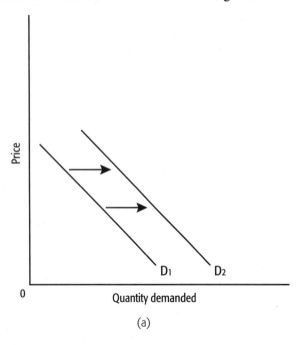

(a)

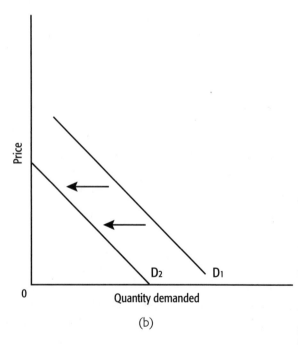

(b)

22. Junior Mints _____

23. Bosco chocolate-flavored syrup _____

24. fried chicken _____

25. yogurt _____

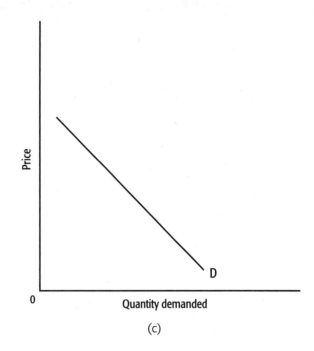

(c)

CHAPTER 4, SECTION 3
Elasticity of Demand

Elasticity Versus Inelasticity

According to the law of demand, when price rises, quantity demanded falls and when price falls, quantity demanded rises. Elasticity of demand is a measure of *how much* the quantity demanded of a good rises or falls due to a change in the price of the good.

You can think of elastic demand as being like an elastic band—the quantity demanded of the good will stretch freely when pulled by a change in the good's price. Inelastic demand is more like a rope—the quantity demanded of the good will not stretch easily when pulled by a change in the good's price.

In questions 1 and 2, circle the letter of the correct answer.

1. If the price of a good with elastic demand increases, which of the following describes the effect on the quantity demanded of the good?

   a. increases a little

   b. increases a lot

   c. decreases a little

   d. decreases a lot

2. If the price of a good with inelastic demand increases, which of the following describes the effect on the quantity demanded of the good?

   a. increases a little

   b. increases a lot

   c. decreases a little

   d. decreases a lot

Factors That Determine Elasticity of Demand

In questions 3–6, list the four factors that determine the elasticity of demand. For each factor, describe how the factor affects the elasticity of demand for a good (that is, explain whether it causes demand to be more elastic or more inelastic).

3. *Factor:*

   _____

   Description:

   _____

   _____

4. *Factor:*

   _____

Description:

_____

_____

5. *Factor:*

_____

Description:

_____

_____

6. *Factor:*

_____

Description:

_____

_____

Considering the factors you listed in questions 3–6, identify the demand for the goods in questions 7–9 as elastic, inelastic, or unit-elastic. Explain the reason for each choice.

7. T-bone steak

_____

_____

8. new sport utility vehicle

_____

_____

9. insulin

_____

_____

In each of the cases described in questions 10–12, identify whether the demand for the good is elastic, inelastic, or unit-elastic. Write your answers on the lines provided.

10. _____ The price of corn rises 5 percent, and the quantity demanded falls 15 percent.

11. _____ The price of bagels rises 8 percent, and the quantity demanded falls 8 percent.

12. _____ The price of telephones rises 10 percent, and the quantity demanded falls 2 percent.

Elasticity and Total Revenue

Elasticity of demand matters to sellers of goods because it relates to their total revenue (Price × Quantity sold = Total revenue). Questions 13–19 relate to how the elasticity of demand for a good affects a seller's total revenue when the seller changes the price of the good. Fill in each blank with the correct answer.

13. If demand for a good is *elastic* and price increases, then total revenue will

    _____.

14. If demand for a good is *elastic* and price decreases, then total revenue will

    _____.

15. If demand for a good is *inelastic* and price increases, then total revenue will

    _____.

16. If demand for a good is *inelastic* and price decreases, then total revenue will

    _____.

17. If demand for a good is *unit-elastic* and price increases, then total revenue will

    _____.

18. If demand for a good is *unit-elastic* and price decreases, then total revenue will

    _____.

19. If a seller would like to increase revenue, the seller should (a) increase the price of the good if the demand for the good is _____ or (b) decrease the price of the good if the demand for the good is _____.

In each of questions 20–22, complete the table to calculate the total revenue for the good. Then fill in the blanks in the question following the table to summarize the results in each case.

20. When Edith increased the price of a good from $2 to $3, the quantity demanded rose from 100 to 110.

	Price	×	Quantity sold	=	Total revenue
Original	$_____		_____		$_____
New	$_____		_____		$_____

    So, because revenue _____ when the price _____, demand for the good must be _____.

21. When Renaldo increased the price from $10 to $12, the quantity demanded fell from 80 to 40.

	Price	×	Quantity sold	=	Total revenue
Original	$_____		_____		$_____
New	$_____		_____		$_____

    So, because revenue _____ when the price _____, demand for the good must be _____.

22. When Keiko decreased the price from $150 to $125, the quantity demanded rose from 60 to 120.

	Price	×	Quantity sold	=	Total revenue
Original	$_____		_____		$_____
New	$_____		_____		$_____

So, because revenue _____ when the price _____, demand

for the good must be _____.

Elasticity of Demand and a Cigarette User Fee

To increase state revenue and decrease smoking rates, the governor of Minnesota proposed that the state impose a $0.75 per pack "cigarette user fee." His proposal was passed by the state legislature. Use this information and your knowledge about elasticity of demand to answer questions 23–26.

23. Did the governor of Minnesota assume that demand for cigarettes was elastic or inelastic when he made his proposal? Explain your answer.

_____

_____

_____

24. Given the large increase in price, in which income groups and age groups would you expect to see the greatest decrease in quantity demanded?

_____

_____

_____

25. Which of the four factors that determine elasticity of demand do you think plays the largest role in people's demand for cigarettes?

_____

_____

_____

26. How might time affect this scenario?

_____

_____

_____

Elasticity of Demand and Gas Prices

Many people once believed that an increase in the price of gasoline would change consumer attitudes and driving behavior. For instance, economists assumed that people would drive less often and buy smaller, more efficient cars as the price of gasoline increased. However, gas prices increased in 2005, and while the sales of sport utility vehicles suffered, people's driving habits and gas consumption levels changed very little. Use this information and your knowledge about elasticity of demand to answer questions 27–29.

27. Is the demand for gasoline more elastic or more inelastic than previously thought? Explain your answer.

_____

_____

_____

28. Which of the four factors that determine elasticity of demand do you think plays the largest role in people's buying habits for gasoline?

_____

_____

_____

29. How might time affect this scenario?

_____

_____

Elasticity of Demand in Graphs

In questions 30 and 31, use your understanding of elasticity of demand to decide whether the graph shows a good with elastic demand or a good with inelastic demand.

30. _____

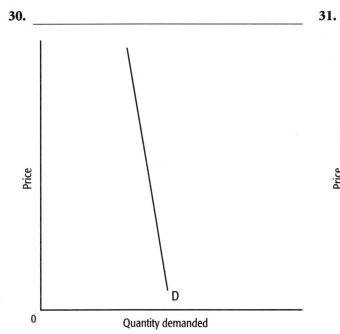

31. _____

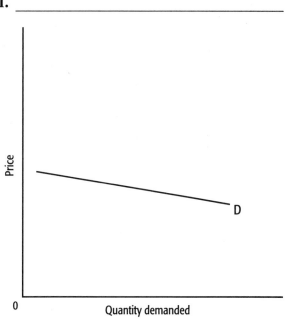

Name: _____ Date: _____

CHAPTER 4

We Demand Practice!

In each of questions 1–14, an event has occurred that will affect the demand or quantity demanded for a good. Illustrate the change in demand or quantity demanded for the good that is listed below the graph. To illustrate a change in demand (also called a shift of the demand curve), draw a parallel line to the right or left of the original line plus an arrow to indicate direction of the shift. To illustrate a change in the quantity demanded (also called a movement along the demand curve), indicate two points on the demand curve and draw an arrow pointing up or down the curve between the two points.

1. Harry Potter movies increase interest in the books.

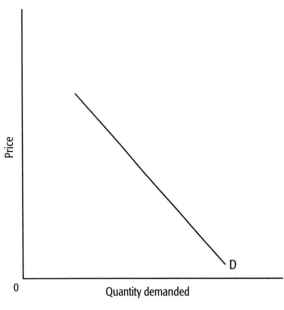

Harry Potter Books

2. Gas prices have risen to new high levels.

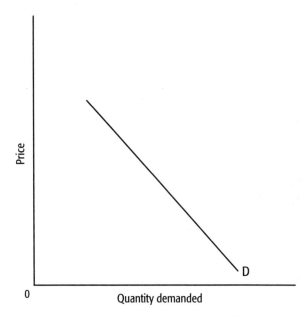

Motor Scooters with High Miles per Gallon

Applying the Principles Workbook   © EMC Publishing

3. The price of beef is expected to rise next week.

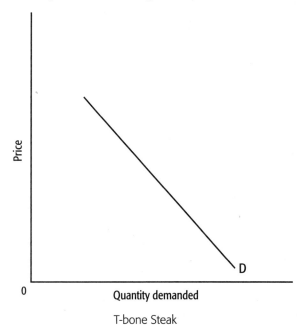

T-bone Steak

4. The price of beef rises.

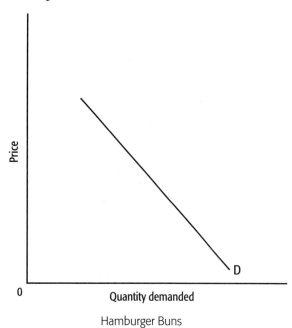

Hamburger Buns

5. The first snowstorm of the season occurs.

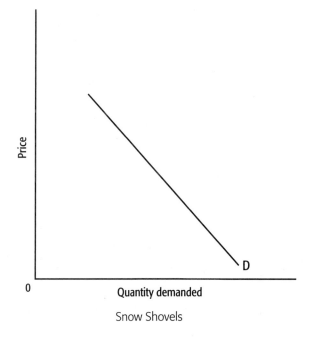

Snow Shovels

6. Summer vacation begins!

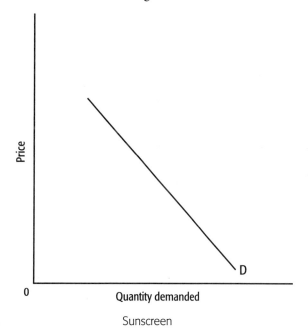

Sunscreen

7. A tax rebate increases incomes.

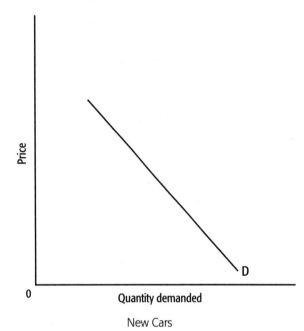

New Cars

8. The price of pork rises.

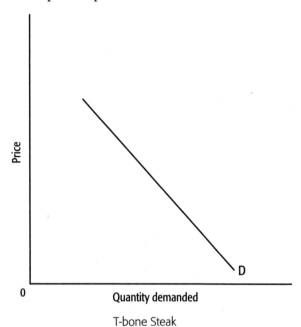

T-bone Steak

9. The price of DVD players decreases.

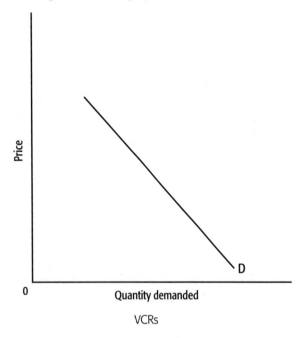

VCRs

10. The price of DVD players decreases.

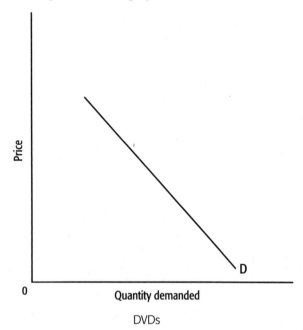

DVDs

11. The price of breakfast cereal rises.

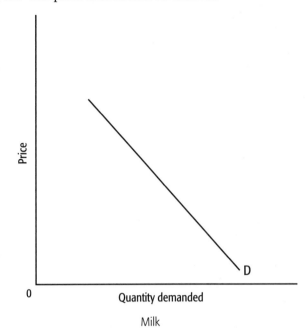

Milk

12. The price of orange juice rises.

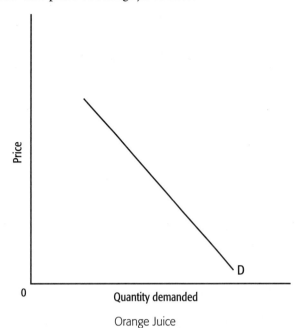

Orange Juice

13. The price of orange juice rises.

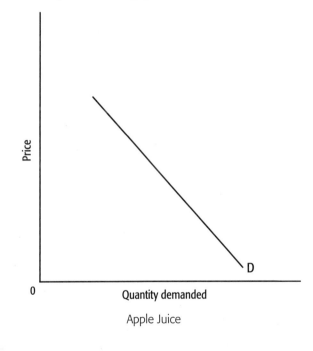

Apple Juice

14. Tiger Woods creates a new fad: golf.

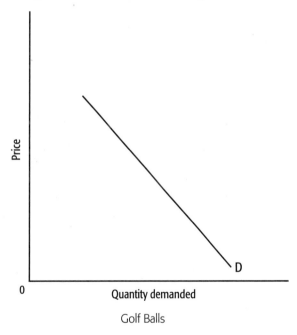

Golf Balls

Name: _____ Date: _____

CHAPTER 5, SECTION 1
Supply!

Supply and the Law of Supply

To be sure you understand supply and the law of supply, fill in the blanks in questions 1–4.

1. The two conditions of supply are _____ and
   _____.

2. The law of supply says that as the price of a good increases, the quantity supplied of the good
   _____.

3. The law of supply says that as the price of a good decreases, the quantity supplied of the good
   _____.

4. According to the law of supply, price and quantity supplied move in _____
   direction(s).

Supply Schedules and Supply Curves

The law of supply can be represented in numbers using a **supply schedule** or it can be
represented as a graph showing a **supply curve**.

Answer question 5 to illustrate the connection between a supply schedule and a supply curve.

5. Simon, an enthusiastic consumer of music
   downloads, has taken a keen interest in the
   industry. He has started his own company,
   Simon, Inc., which manufactures premium
   mp3 players. Use the supply schedule below to
   create a supply curve for Simon's company on
   the grid shown. Label the curve S_1.

SUPPLY SCHEDULE FOR SIMON, INC.

Price (dollars)	Quantity demanded (units)
$100	200
$200	300
$300	400
$400	500
$500	600
$600	700
$700	800

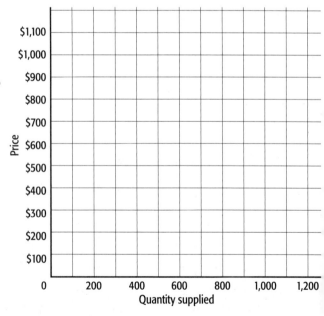

Supply Curve Derived from Supply Schedule

Applying the Principles Workbook © EMC Publishing

Use the graph you created in question 5 to answer questions 6–8.

6. The supply curve shows that at a price of $300, Simon, Inc., will offer to sell _____ premium mp3 players, and at a price of $600, the company will offer to sell _____ premium mp3 players.

7. The company's selling behavior demonstrates the law of _____.

8. The change in production of Simon, Inc., at different prices is a change in _____.

All producers do not supply the same amount of a good. Some are willing and able to supply greater quantities than others are.

Use the information in question 9 to compare the supply curves of two different companies for the same good.

9. Use the supply schedule below to create a supply curve for premium mp3 players for Carla, Inc. Draw the graph on the grid in question 5. Label the curve S_2.

SUPPLY SCHEDULE FOR CARLA, INC.

Price (dollars)	Quantity supplied (units)
$100	400
$200	500
$300	600
$400	700
$500	800
$600	900
$700	1,000

To answer questions 10–14, use the graph in question 5, which now shows the supply curves for both Simon, Inc., and Carla, Inc.

10. The supply curve for Carla, Inc., (S_2) is to the _____ of the supply curve for Simon, Inc., (S_1).

11. For each of the listed prices, Carla, Inc., is willing and able to produce _____ premium mp3 players than Simon, Inc., is willing and able to produce.

12. At each of the possible quantities, Carla, Inc., is willing to accept a _____ price than Simon, Inc., is willing to accept.

13. The supply curves you created on the grid in question 5 are _____ supply curves.

14. Suppose Simon, Inc., and Carla, Inc., are the only suppliers of premium mp3 players. How would you create a market supply curve from the supply curves you drew on the grid in question 5?

_____

_____

_____

Vertical Supply Curves

As shown in the figure to the right, a supply curve is vertical when the quantity supplied cannot increase regardless of the price. For instance, the number of tickets available for this season's Super Bowl is finite because the stadium has a fixed number of seats. A vertical supply curve illustrates that at any price, the quantity supplied remains the same.

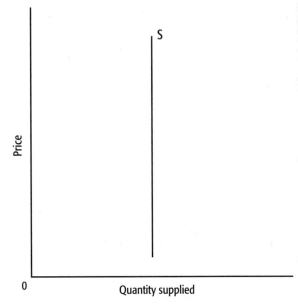

Supply Curve When Quantity Supplied Cannot Increase

Write your answer to question 15 on the lines provided.

15. List three other goods that would have vertical supply curves.

_____

_____

CHAPTER 5, SECTION 2

The Supply Curve Shifts

Changes in Supply and Shifts in Supply Curves

When supply changes, the supply curve shifts. Fill in the blanks in questions 1 and 2 with the correct answers.

1. If supply increases, the supply curve shifts ___right___, meaning that sellers want to sell ___more___ of a good at each and every price.

2. If supply decreases, the supply curve shifts ___left___, meaning that sellers want to sell ___less___ of a good at each and every price.

Factors That Cause Shifts in Demand Curves

In questions 3–10, list the factors that cause supply curves to shift. For each factor, describe how the factor affects the supply of a good (whether the factor causes supply to rise or to fall).

3. *Factor:*

   ___Resource Prices___

   Description:

   → ___When resources prices fall, supplies increase because goods are cheaper to produce___

4. *Factor:*

   ___Technology___

   Description:

   → ___If technology advances, then supply increases because production becomes easier and cheaper___

5. *Factor:*

   ___Taxes___

   Description:

   ← ___If taxes increase on production, then there is less supply because cost per-unit can rise___

6. *Factor:*

Subsidies

Description:

→ supply increases with subsidy because they get money for production

7. *Factor:*

Quotas

Description:

← decreases supply because it is a limit put on imports

8. *Factor:*

Number of Sellers

Description:

→ if more sellers produce the good then supply rises

9. *Factor:*

Future Price

Description:

←→ if they think prices will rise ~~later~~ later then they will hold off so supply is low. If price will drop later they will increase supply now.

10. *Factor:*

Weather

Description:

←→ (agricultur) good weather = more supply
bad weather = less supply

Supply Versus Quantity Supplied

Supply is not the same as quantity supplied. Answer questions 11–14 on the lines provided.

11. What will cause a change in the supply of a good?

_____

_____

12. What will cause a change in the quantity supplied of a good?

_____

_____

13. How is a change in supply represented on a graph?

_____

_____

14. How is a change in quantity supplied represented on a graph?

_____

_____

Changes in Supply and in Quantity Supplied

In questions 15–23, fill in the blanks to describe how each event will affect the country's total supply of corn.

15. The U.S. government increases the subsidy for corn production.

Will the supply of corn increase, decrease, or stay the same?

_____

In which direction will the supply curve shift?

_____

Which of the eight factors causes the shift?

_____

16. A major drought destroys crops in America's heartland.

Will the supply of corn increase, decrease, or stay the same?

_____

In which direction will the supply curve shift?

_____

Which of the eight factors causes the shift?

_____

17. The price of fuel used in farm machinery increases to a new high.

Will the supply of corn increase, decrease, or stay the same?

_____

In which direction will the supply curve shift?

_____

Which of the eight factors causes the shift?

_____

18. The U.S. government places a quota on all imported farm products.

Will the supply of corn increase, decrease, or stay the same?

_____

In which direction will the supply curve shift?

_____

Which of the eight factors causes the shift?

_____

19. A newly developed seed increases the corn yield.

Will the supply of corn increase, decrease, or stay the same?

_____

In which direction will the supply curve shift?

_____

Which of the eight factors causes the shift?

_____

20. As property values rise, many farm fields are turned into housing developments and shopping malls.

Will the supply of corn increase, decrease, or stay the same?

_____

In which direction will the supply curve shift?

_____

Which of the eight factors causes the shift?

_____

21. The U.S. government gives farmers a tax cut by allowing them to deduct most expenses.

Will the supply of corn increase, decrease, or stay the same?

_____

In which direction will the supply curve shift?

_____

Which of the eight factors causes the shift?

_____

22. Corn prices are expected to rise next month as more ethanol refineries start production.

Will the supply of corn increase, decrease, or stay the same?

_____

In which direction will the supply curve shift?

_____

Which of the eight factors causes the shift?

_____

23. Chocolate-covered corn on a stick becomes a new fad at state fairs.

Will the supply of corn increase, decrease, or stay the same?

_____

In which direction will the supply curve shift?

_____

Which of the eight factors causes the shift?

_____

Elasticity of Supply

Elasticity of supply is a measure of *how much* the quantity supplied of a good rises or falls owing to a change in the price of the good.

Fill in the blanks in questions 24–26 with the correct answers.

24. When quantity supplied changes by a larger percentage than price, supply is _____.

25. When quantity supplied changes by a smaller percentage than price, supply is

_____.

26. When quantity supplied changes by the same percentage as price, supply is _____.

Elasticity Versus Inelasticity

In each of the cases described in questions 27–29, identify whether the supply of the good is elastic, inelastic, or unit-elastic.

27. _____ The price of textbooks increases by 20 percent, and the quantity supplied of textbooks rises 20 percent.

28. _____ The price of jeans increases by 5 percent, and the quantity supplied of jeans increases by 3 percent.

29. _____ The price of televisions increases by 15 percent, and the quantity supplied of televisions increases by 25 percent.

In questions 30 and 31, use your understanding of elasticity of supply to decide whether the graph shows a good with elastic supply or a good with inelastic supply.

30. _____

31. _____

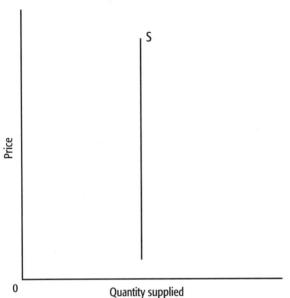

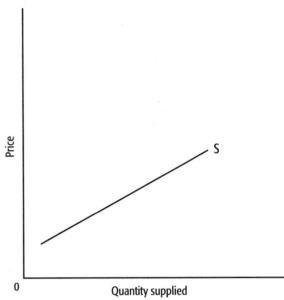

Write your answers to questions 32 and 33 on the lines provided.

32. The supply of some goods, such as houses, increases at a slow pace. Do you think the supply of houses is more elastic in the short run or in the long run?

_____

_____

_____

33. Will the supply curve for most goods become more vertical or more horizontal as time passes?

_____

_____

_____

CHAPTER 5

Supply Practice!

In each of questions 1–14, an event has occurred that will affect the supply or quantity supplied of a good. Illustrate the change in supply or quantity supplied for the good that is listed below the graph. To illustrate a change in supply (also called a shift of the supply curve), draw a parallel line to the right or left of the original line, plus an arrow to indicate the direction of the shift. To illustrate a change in the quantity supplied (also called a movement along the supply curve), indicate two points on the supply curve, and draw an arrow pointing up or down the curve between the two points.

1. Soybean prices are expected to rise next month.

2. The government decides to subsidize oil companies.

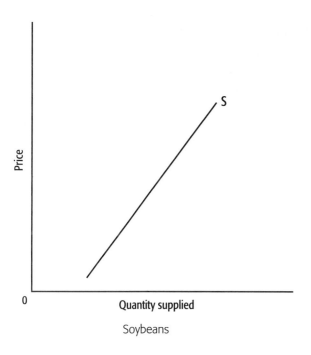

Soybeans

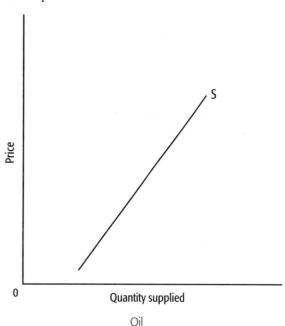

Oil

3. The autoworkers union wins higher pay for workers.

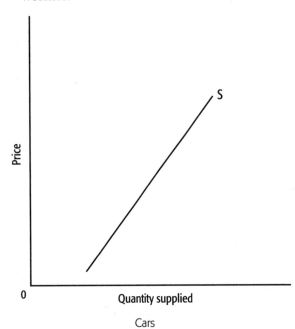

Cars

4. The government places a quota on imported textiles.

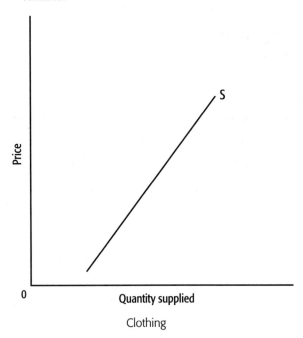

Clothing

5. Storms ruin citrus crops in Florida.

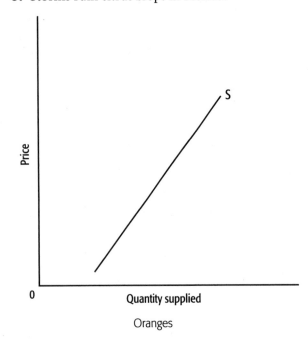

Oranges

6. Steel prices soar.

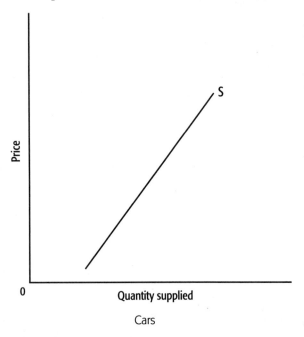

Cars

7. Paper prices fall.

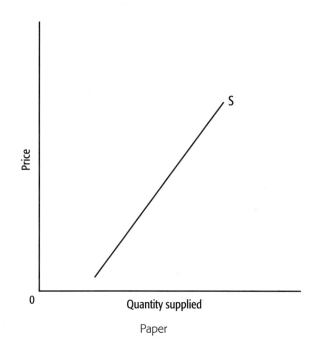

Paper

8. Government increases the tax that cigarette producers pay.

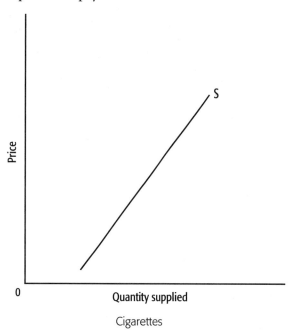

Cigarettes

9. New software increases widget production.

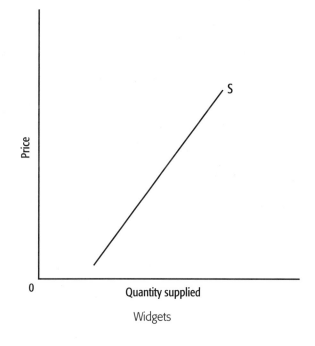

Widgets

10. The price of wheat is expected to fall next week.

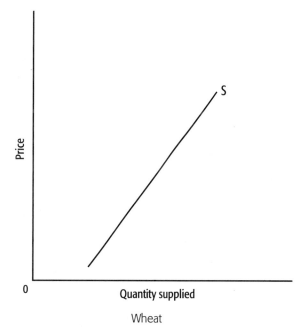

Wheat

11. A new trade agreement eliminates sugar quotas.

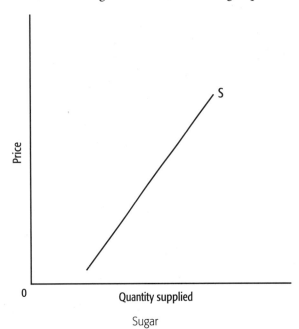

Sugar

12. Lumber prices rise.

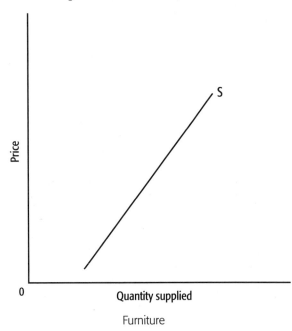

Furniture

13. High profits increase the number of cell phone manufacturers.

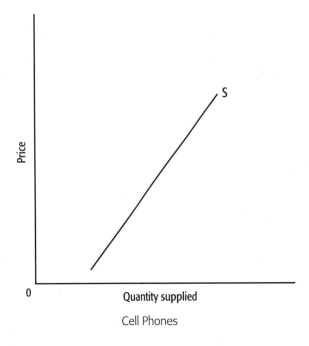

Cell Phones

14. Computer producers outsource jobs to reduce labor costs.

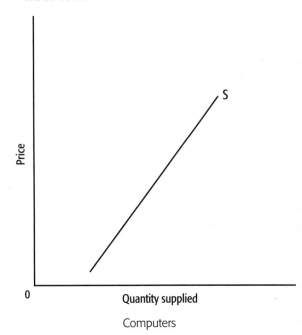

Computers

CHAPTER 6, SECTION 1

Price: Supply and Demand Together

In a market, supply and demand work together to determine the price of a good. Write your answers to questions 1–6 in the blanks provided to be sure you understand the different market conditions and how they affect price.

1. What market condition exists when quantity supplied is greater than quantity demanded?

   Surplus

2. What happens to price when the market condition in question 1 exists? *prices will lower*

3. What market condition exists when quantity demanded is greater than quantity supplied?

   shortage

4. What happens to price when the market condition in question 3 exists? *prices will rise*

5. What market condition exists when quantity demanded is equal to quantity supplied?

   equlibrium

6. Do markets tend to move toward shortage, surplus, or equilibrium? *equilibrium*

Suppose that in the market for gadgets, the quantities demanded and supplied at various prices are as shown in the following table, and answer question 7.

SUPPLY AND DEMAND IN THE GADGET MARKET

Price	Quantity Demanded	Quantity Supplied
$0.10	450	50
$0.20	400	100
$0.30	350	150
$0.40	300	200
$0.50	250	250
$0.60	200	300
$0.70	150	350
$0.80	100	400

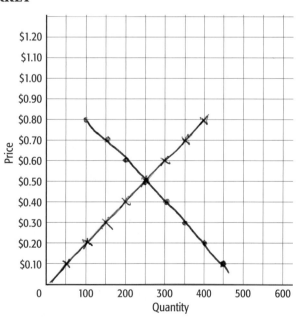

Price: Supply and Demand Together

7. Use the information in the table to draw the supply and demand curves for the gadget market on the following grid. Label the vertical axis "Price" and label the horizontal axis "Quantity." Use the prices and quantities demanded in the table to plot the demand curve. Label it D_1. Use the prices and quantities supplied in the table to plot the supply curve. Label it S_1.

Use the graph you created in question 7 to answer questions 8–15.

8. The equilibrium price in the gadget market is _____.

9. At the equilibrium price, sellers want to sell _____ gadgets and buyers want to buy _____ gadgets.

10. If the price of gadgets rises to $0.70, sellers will want to sell _____ gadgets and buyers will want to buy _____ gadgets.

11. A price rise to $0.70 will result in a _____ of _____ gadgets.

12. If the market condition in question 11 exists, prices will _____ and price will settle at _____.

13. If the price of gadgets falls to $0.30, sellers will want to sell _____ gadgets and buyers will want to buy _____ gadgets.

14. A price fall to $0.30 will result in a _____ of _____ gadgets.

15. If the market condition in question 13 exists, prices will _____ and price will settle at _____.

Now assume that as a result of changing consumer preferences, gadgets become the newest fad, and respond to questions 16 and 17.

16. Will this change in consumer preferences cause a change in demand or quantity demanded?

_____

17. Use the demand schedule below to draw a second demand curve on the grid in question 7. Label this second demand curve D_2.

Price	Quantity demanded
$0.10	550
$0.20	500
$0.30	450
$0.40	400
$0.50	350
$0.60	300
$0.70	250
$0.80	200

Use the graph in question 7, which now shows demand curves D_1 and D_2 and supply curve S_1, to answer questions 18–21.

18. The new equilibrium price in the gadget market is _____.

19. At the new price, sellers want to sell _____ gadgets and buyers want to buy _____ gadgets.

20. Is the gadget market described by D_2 and S_1 in a state of shortage, surplus, or equilibrium?

_____

21. So, as a result of the change in consumer preferences, the price of gadgets increased _____, the quantity demanded increased _____ units, and the quantity supplied increased _____ units.

Price is a way for buyers and sellers to communicate with each other. It signals a change in the market for a good. Fill in each blank in questions 22–25 with the correct word.

22. When a market experiences a shortage, price will _____.

23. When a shortage occurs, supply and demand work together to influence price and move the market toward _____.

24. When a market experiences a surplus, price will _____.

25. When a surplus occurs, supply and demand work together to influence price and move the market toward _____.

CHAPTER 6, SECTION 1
Price Controls

Fill in the blanks in questions 1 and 2 with the correct words.

1. A price ceiling is a legislated price _____ which legal trades cannot be made.

2. A price floor is a legislated price _____ which legal trades cannot be made.

Rent control is a price ceiling. It is an effort by local government to help the poor by making housing more affordable. The following graph shows apartment rents in a local housing market.

Use the graph to answer questions 3 and 4.

3. The equilibrium price of apartments in this market is _____.

4. The equilibrium quantity of apartments in this market is _____ units.

Now suppose this local government imposes rent controls that require apartments be rented for no more than $600, and respond to question 5.

5. Draw a horizontal line across the graph at a price (rent) of $600 to show this price ceiling.

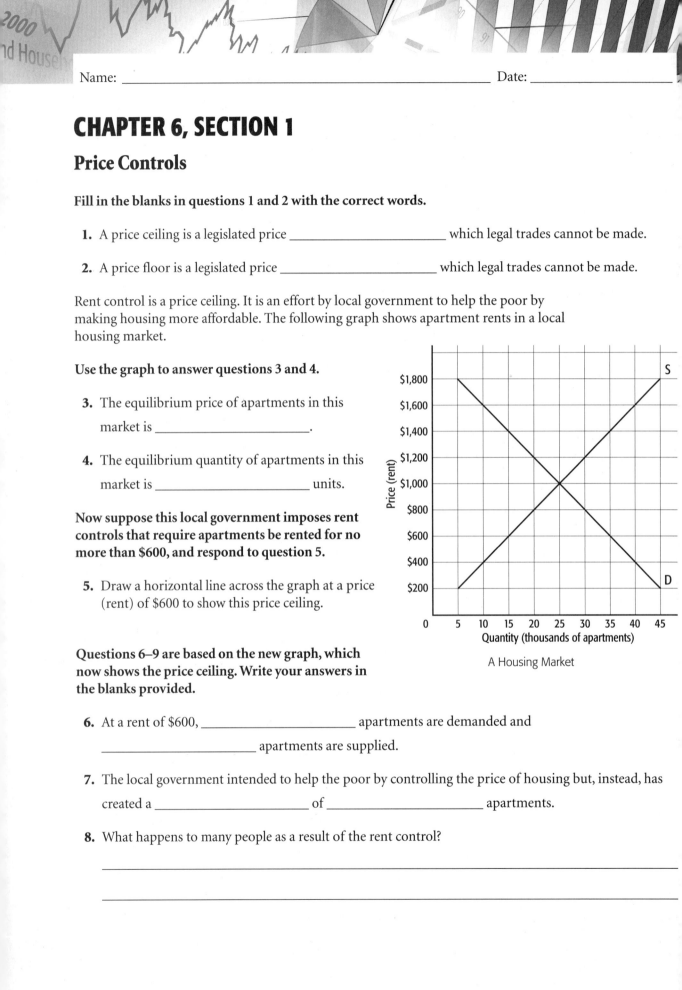

A Housing Market

Questions 6–9 are based on the new graph, which now shows the price ceiling. Write your answers in the blanks provided.

6. At a rent of $600, _____ apartments are demanded and _____ apartments are supplied.

7. The local government intended to help the poor by controlling the price of housing but, instead, has created a _____ of _____ apartments.

8. What happens to many people as a result of the rent control?

   _____

   _____

9. How could the local government achieve its goal of helping the poor without using rent control?

_____

_____

A minimum wage is a price floor. It is an effort by state or federal government to ensure that workers receive a fair wage for their labor. The following graph shows the wages in a labor market.

Use the graph to answer questions 10 and 11.

10. The equilibrium price of labor in this market is

_____.

11. The equilibrium quantity of labor in this market

is _____ workers.

Now, suppose that government imposes a minimum wage of $8 an hour—no worker can receive a wage of less than $8 an hour—and answer question 12.

12. Draw a horizontal line across the graph at a price (wage) of $8 to show this price floor.

A Labor Market

Questions 13–16 are based on the new graph, which now shows the price floor. Write your answers in the blanks provided.

13. At a wage of $8 an hour, _____ workers are demanded and

_____ workers are supplied.

14. Government intended to help workers by setting a minimum wage but, instead, has created a

_____ of _____ workers.

15. What happens to many workers as a result of the minimum wage? _____.

16. How could government achieve its goal of helping workers without using a minimum wage?

_____

_____

Write your answers to questions 17 and 18 in the blanks provided.

17. If economists generally oppose price controls because of their negative unintended effects, why do you think politicians continue to use them?

_____

_____

_____

_____

18. As a worker who likely would benefit from an increase in the minimum wage, how do you feel about proposals to raise the minimum wage?

_____

_____

_____

In August of 2005, Hawaii passed a law to control the price of gasoline. The law was meant to protect people from suspected price gouging by controlling the maximum price wholesalers could charge for gasoline.

Write your answers to questions 19–21 in the blanks provided.

19. The Hawaiian law is a _____.

20. Hawaii will likely experience a _____ of gasoline as a result of the law.

21. If a legislator in Hawaii asked your opinion about the gasoline price control, what would you say?

_____

_____

_____

_____

CHAPTER 6, SECTION 2

Supply and Demand in Everyday Life

Each of the graphs in questions 1–9 shows supply and demand for the good named in the title of the graph. Then the event described occurs. On the graph, illustrate the shift in the supply curve or the demand curve as a result of the event. Then, fill in the blanks to indicate how equilibrium price and equilibrium quantity change as a result of the event.

1. *Event:* The price of snow skis goes up.

   The equilibrium price of ski boots goes _____ and the equilibrium quantity of ski boots goes _____.

2. *Event:* The Atkins low-carb diet sweeps the nation.

   The equilibrium price of hamburger goes _____ and the equilibrium quantity of hamburger goes _____.

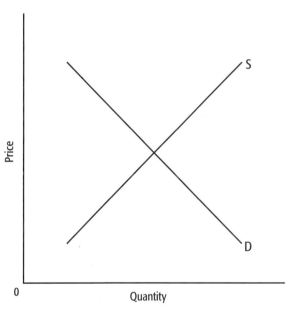

Supply and Demand for Ski Boots

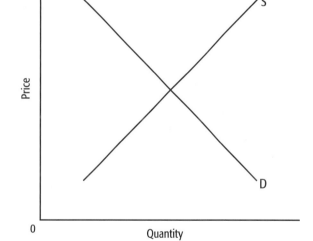

Supply and Demand for Hamburger

3. *Event:* New technologies are introduced in the gadget-manufacturing process.
The equilibrium price of gadgets goes

_____ and the

equilibrium quantity of gadgets goes

_____.

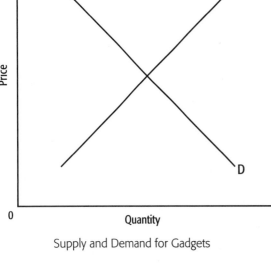

Supply and Demand for Gadgets

4. *Event:* The U.S. government imposes a quota to protect the domestic steel industry.
The equilibrium price of American-made cars

goes _____ and the

equilibrium quantity of American-made cars

goes _____.

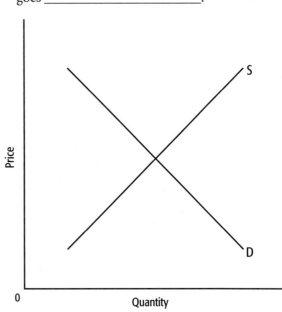

Supply and Demand for American-Made Cars

5. *Event:* The price of DVD players drops.
The equilibrium price of VHS tapes goes

_____ and the

equilibrium quantity of VHS tapes goes

_____.

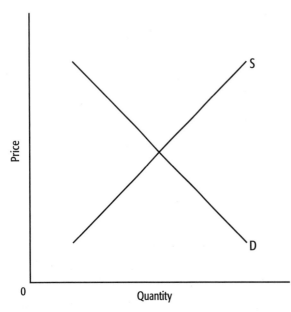

Supply and Demand for VHS Tapes

6. *Event:* Petroleum refineries are put out of commission due to a hurricane.
The equilibrium price of gasoline goes

_____ and the

equilibrium quantity of gasoline goes

_____.

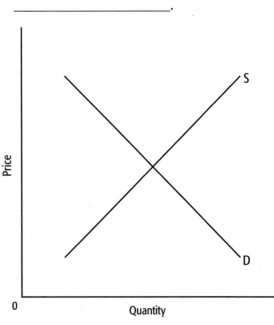

Supply and Demand for Gasoline

7. *Event:* The government increases the amount of the corn subsidy paid to farmers.

The equilibrium price of corn goes

_____ and the

equilibrium quantity of corn goes

_____.

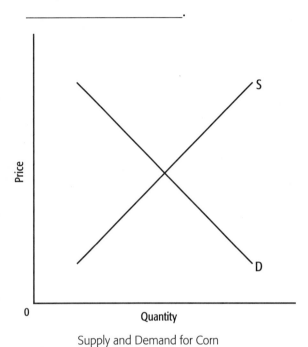

Supply and Demand for Corn

8. *Event:* Consumers expect the price of gasoline to increase tomorrow.

The equilibrium price of gasoline goes

_____ and the

equilibrium quantity of gasoline goes

_____.

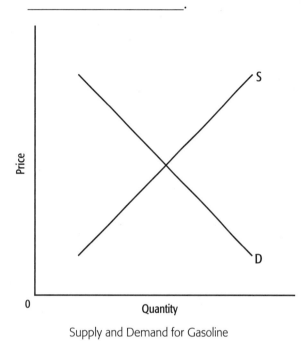

Supply and Demand for Gasoline

9. *Event:* Coffee prices increase.

The equilibrium price of tea goes

_____ and the

equilibrium quantity of tea goes

_____.

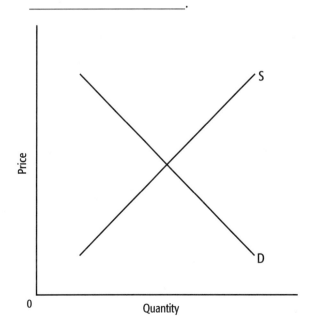

Supply and Demand for Tea As Replacement for Coffee

The following graph shows the market for the reunion tour of a famous 1980s rock band. Use the graph to answer questions 10–15.

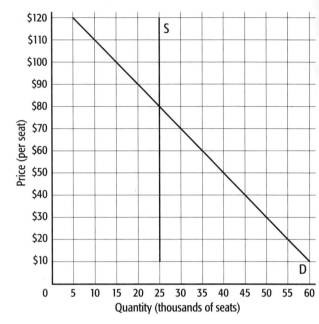

Ticket Price for Famous 1980s Rock Band Concert

10. The equilibrium price is _____.

11. The equilibrium quantity is _____ tickets.

12. Why is the supply curve vertical?

    _____

    _____

13. If concert organizers decide to charge $100 per ticket, the result will be a _____
    of _____ tickets.

14. If concert organizers decide to charge $60 per ticket, the result will be a _____ of
    _____ tickets.

15. Ticket scalpers will exist only if tickets are priced below _____.

Name: _____ Date: _____

CHAPTER 7, SECTION 1
About Business Firms

Necessity of Bosses

Write your answers to questions 1 and 2 in the blanks provided.

1. The following events are not listed in the order in which they are likely to occur. Number the events in chronological order from 1 to 5.

   _____ The monitor is made a residual claimant.

   _____ Increased shirking reduces the output of the firm.

   _____ Firm comes into existence.

   _____ A monitor is chosen.

   _____ People in the firm start to shirk.

2. A monitor may be made a residual claimant. How will this prevent the monitor from shirking?

   _____

   _____

Types of Firms

In questions 3–17, identify the type of firm (sole proprietorship, partnership, or corporation) that best answers the question.

3. Which type of firm has limited liability?

   _____

4. Which type of firm is likely to have the greatest number of owners?

   _____

5. Which types of firms have unlimited liability?

   _____

6. Which type of firm suffers from double taxation?

   _____

7. Which type of firm has only one owner?

   _____

8. Which type of firm is likely to have the shortest life span?

   _____

9. Which type of firm is the easiest to form and to dissolve?

_____

10. Which type of firm is owned by stockholders?

_____

11. In which type of firm does a board of directors make the important decisions?

_____

12. In which type of firm is decision making often the easiest?

_____

13. Barbershops and restaurants are examples of which type of firm?

_____

14. Law firms and medical offices are examples of which type of firm?

_____

15. Wal-Mart, Best Buy, and General Electric are examples of which type of firm?

_____

16. Which type of firm accounts for the greatest number of firms?

_____

17. Which type of firm accounts for the greatest number of receipts (sales)?

_____

Double taxation is considered to be a disadvantage of corporations. Write your answers to questions 18–20 in the blanks provided.

18. Explain double taxation.

_____

_____

_____

19. Is it fair to tax corporate profits twice?

_____

_____

20. Some people argue that either the corporate income tax or the income tax on dividends should be reduced or eliminated. What might be some of the effects of reducing or eliminating one or both of these taxes? (*Hint:* Consider the circular flow diagram of economic activity in the U.S. economy—Exhibit 3-2 on page 60 of your text.)

_____

_____

_____

_____

_____

Corporations, like all firms, can raise money by borrowing from banks and other lending institutions. However, corporations also can raise money by selling bonds or issuing additional shares of stock.

In questions 21–24, identify the type of financing (stock or bond) that best answers the question.

21. In which form of corporate financing is the investor a lender to the corporation?

_____

22. In which form of corporate financing is the investor also an owner? _____

23. Which form of corporate financing involves more risk for the investor? _____

24. Which form of corporate financing involves the potential for greater returns for the investor?

_____

Franchises

Write your answers to questions 25–27 in the blanks provided.

25. Franchises have become more common in the last 25 years. What are the advantages and disadvantages of buying a franchise?

Advantages:

_____

_____

Disadvantages:

_____

_____

26. According to Milton Friedman, what is the only social responsibility of business?

_____

_____

_____

27. Do you agree or disagree with Milton Friedman's opposition to businesses donating funds to charitable organizations? Give reasons for your answer.

_____

_____

_____

Applying the Principles Workbook

CHAPTER 7, SECTIONS 2 AND 3

Costs and Revenue

Fill in the blanks in questions 1–6 to be sure you understand some important economic terms.

1. A fixed cost ___*are the same*___ no matter how many units of a good are produced.

2. An example of a fixed cost is ___*insurance payement*___

3. A variable cost ___*changes*___ with the number of units of a good produced.

4. An example of a variable cost is ___*wages of workers*___.

5. In economics, the word ___*marginal*___ means additional, so ___*marginal cost*___ is the cost of producing an additional unit of a good and ___*marginal revenue*___ is the revenue from selling an additional unit of a good.

6. Every firm wants to maximize ___*profit*___.

Complete the cost and revenue formulas in questions 7–12.

7. Total cost (TC) =
   Fixed costs + variable costs

   △ = change in

8. Average total cost (ATC) = $\dfrac{TC}{Q}$

9. Marginal cost (MC) = $\dfrac{\Delta TC}{\Delta Q}$

10. Total revenue (TR) =
    price of a good (P) × quantity of units (Q) $TR = P \times Q$

11. Marginal revenue (MR) =
    $MR = \dfrac{\Delta TR}{\Delta Q}$

12. Profit (or loss) =
    $TR - TC$

13. Use the formulas in questions 7–12 to fill in the missing numbers in the following table. For this firm, marginal revenue is the same as price.

Gadgets/ hour	Fixed cost	Variable cost	Total cost	Marginal cost	Marginal revenue	Total revenue	Profit or (loss)
0	$24	$ 0	$ 24	$ 0	$24	$ 0	($ 24)
1	$24	____	$ 32	$ 8	$24	$ 24	____
2	____	$ 12	$ 36	____	$24	____	$ 12
3	$24	$ 15	____	$ 3	$24	____	$ 33
4	$24	____	$ 44	____	____	$ 96	____
5	$24	____	$ 51	$ 7	$24	____	$ 69
6	$24	$ 36	____	____	$24	$144	____
7	____	$ 48	____	$12	____	$168	____
8	$24	____	$ 87	____	$24	____	$105
9	$24	____	$106	$19	$24	$216	____
10	$24	$106	____	$24	$24	____	$110
11	$24	$136	____	____	____	$264	____
12	____	$173	____	$37	$24	____	$ 91

Total Revenue and Marginal Revenue

Every firm must answer certain questions. One question is: How much should the firm produce? Fill in the blanks in question 14 to answer this question. Then use the table in question 13 to answer questions 15–17.

14. According to economists, a business should continue to produce additional units of its good until

    _____ is equal to _____.

15. So, the firm in question 12 should produce _____ gadgets at current prices.

16. If the price (marginal revenue) of gadgets rises to $37, the firm should produce _____ gadgets.

17. If the price (marginal revenue) of gadgets drops to $15, the firm should produce _____ gadgets.

A firm also needs to decide how many workers to hire. To see how a firm makes this decision, you need to understand the law of diminishing marginal returns. Fill in the blanks in questions 18 and 19 with the correct answers.

18. According to the law of diminishing marginal returns, if additional units of one

    _____, such as labor, are added to another _____ in fixed

    supply, such as capital, eventually the additional output (produced as a result of hiring an additional

    worker) will _____.

19. If a firm adds workers to increase production, more _____ must be added to
    minimize the effects of the law of diminishing marginal returns.

A firm decides how many workers to hire by looking at both the costs and the benefits of an additional worker. The benefits are the additional output produced as a result of hiring an additional worker and the revenue generated by that additional output (price of good produced × additional output). The costs are the additional wages paid to an additional worker.

Based on the above information, answer questions 20-21.

20. According to economists, a firm should hire additional workers until the additional output produced by the additional worker multiplied by the price of the good is _____ the wage the firm must pay the worker.

21. Fill in the missing numbers in the following table.

Number of workers	Quantity of output per hour	Additional output produced by hiring an additional worker	Additional revenue generated if the price of the good is $5
0	0	0	$ 0
1	4	4	$20
2	10	6	$30
3	17	_____	_____
4	23	_____	_____
5	28	_____	_____
6	31	_____	_____
7	32	_____	_____
8	31	_____	_____

Use the table in question 21 to answer questions 22 and 23.

22. The law of diminishing marginal returns sets in with the _____.

23. If the firm pays workers $15 an hour, it should hire _____.

CHAPTER 8, SECTION 1

A Perfectly Competitive Market

In questions 1–4, list the characteristics of a perfectly competitive market.

1. The market has many buyers and many sellers

2. All firms sell identical goods

3. Buyers and sellers have relevant information about prices, product quality, sources of supply, and so on.

4. Firms have easy entry into and exit out of the market

The characteristics of a perfectly competitive market determine certain characteristics of the sellers in the market. Write your answers to questions 5–8 in the blanks provided.

5. A seller in a perfectly competitive market is a price taker. What is a price taker?

   A seller that can ~~only~~ sell all its output at the equilibrium price but can sell none at any other price

6. Why does a price taker take the equilibrium price? Why doesn't he or she sell for a price that is higher or lower than equilibrium?

   They take equilibrium price because they won't sell any above and don't want to sell any below

7. How much output does a seller in a perfectly competitive market produce?

   It produces the quantity of output at which $MR = MC$

Applying the Principles Workbook

8. What price does a seller in a perfectly competitive market charge for its product?

It sells for the equilibrium price determined by the market

9. Fill in the missing numbers in the following table. The data are for a seller in a perfectly competitive market in which the equilibrium price is $15.

Units of output	Total revenue	Marginal revenue	Total cost	Marginal cost	Profit or (loss)
1	$ 15	$15	$21	—	($6)
2	$_____	$15	$29	$ 8	$ 1
3	$ 45	$_____	$33	$ 4	$12
4	$_____	$15	$37	$_____	$23
5	$ 75	$_____	$49	$12	$_____
6	$_____	$15	$64	$_____	$_____
7	$105	$_____	$81	$_____	$_____

Use the table in question 9 to answer questions 10 and 11.

10. How much output should the firm produce? _____

11. What price should the firm charge for its product? _____

Write your answers to questions 12–14 in the blanks provided.

12. In perfectly competitive markets, how does profit act as a signal?

_____

_____

13. What happens in a perfectly competitive market if the firms in the market earn profits?

_____

_____

_____

14. If a law is passed that taxes away the profits earned by firms in a perfectly competitive market, what might be the unintended effect of the tax?

_____

_____

_____

_____

_____

CHAPTER 8, SECTION 2

A Monopolistic Market

Characteristics

In questions 1–3, list the characteristics of a monopolistic market.

1. _____

   _____

2. _____

   _____

3. _____

   _____

The characteristics of a monopolistic market determine certain characteristics of the seller in the market. Write your answers to questions 4–8 in the blanks provided.

4. Whereas a firm in a perfectly competitive market is a price taker, the firm in a monopolistic market is a
   _____searcher_____.

5. For what price does a monopolist search?
   _____price____that____generates the highest profit_____

   _____

6. How does a monopolist know when it has found the right price?
   _____Trial____and____error_____

   _____

7. How much output does a monopolist produce?
   _____MR= MC_____

   _____

8. What price does a monopolist charge for its product?
   _____Highest___price___that____will___sell___all___units

   _____

Price

Questions 9–11 relate to price in a monopolistic market. Write your answers in the blanks provided.

9. Is it easier for a perfectly competitive firm or for a monopolist to determine price? Explain.

perfectly competitive

10. Does a monopolist face any limit on the price it charges? Explain.

Yes has to have the highest price where all output is sold. $ too high = no sale

11. Is a monopolist guaranteed profits? Explain.

No, must sell above the average total cost

Types of Monopolies

Barriers to entry help maintain a monopolist's market position by protecting the monopolist from competition. For each of the barriers listed in questions 12–16, identify the type of monopoly—government or market—that results from the barrier. Then describe how the barrier limits competition.

12. public franchise

Type of monopoly:

Government

Description:

Eliminates competition by law

13. extremely low average total costs

Type of monopoly:

market

Description:

lower per-unit cost. cant be beaten

14. patent

Type of monopoly:

Government

Description: .

Inventors can claim their own invention

15. copyright

Type of monopoly:

Government

Description:

16. exclusive ownership of a scarce resource

Type of monopoly:

Market

Description:

In each of questions 17–20, identify the company described as a government monopoly or a market monopoly.

17. Company A owns nearly all of the world's diamonds.

_____

18. Company B invents an entirely new product, and a patent is granted.

_____

19. Company C has the exclusive right to provide cable TV services to a city.

_____

20. Company D has per-unit costs that are much lower than those of any of its competitors.

_____

Laws

Each of the scenarios in questions 21–25 presents a monopoly issue. In each blank provided, write the name of the law that was passed to deal with the issue.

21. Company A, a nationally known "big box" store with 150,000 square feet of merchandise, builds a store in your city. Because company A buys from suppliers in huge quantities, it receives special discounts. The small businesses in town say they are unable to survive and must have protection from company A.

_____

22. People in your town have been flocking to company W since it started its new advertising campaign. The company is making claims that seem too good to be true. The competitors of company W say that company W is using false advertising to deceive its customers.

_____

23. Company X promises to sell a scarce resource to company B only if company B buys other goods from company X.

_____

24. Company Y attempts to buy all the firms that compete with it.

_____

25. Your chief competitor, company Z, slashes prices on its products. Its new prices are much lower than the prices charged by any of its competitors in town. You and the other business owners in town accuse company Z of cutthroat pricing.

_____

CHAPTER 8, SECTION 3

A Monopolistic Competitive Market

Characteristics

In questions 1–3, list the characteristics of a monopolistic competitive market.

1. ~~Market consists of one seller~~ many buyers and sellers

2. ~~Product has~~ no close substitute & slightly different

3. The barriers to entry are ~~high~~ ~~low~~

The characteristics of a monopolistic competitive market determine certain characteristics of the sellers in the market. Write your answers to questions 4 and 5 in the blanks provided.

4. How much output does a monopolistic competitor produce?

   $MR = MC$

5. What price does a monopolistic competitor charge for its product?

   The charge whatever is at the height of the demand curve, Highest price at which all units can be sold

Competition and Product

Questions 6 and 7 relate to the amount of competition a seller faces. Write your answers in the blanks provided.

6. Do most sellers prefer more competition or less competition? Explain why.

   less competition because they would maximi sales

7. What two factors determine the amount of competition a seller faces?

   How close to unique a seller's product is, how easy it is for new sellers to enter

Applying the Principles Workbook

Although two of the characteristics of monopolistic competition are the same as characteristics of perfect competition, unlike firms in perfectly competitive markets, monopolistic competitors sell slightly different products.

Write your answers to questions 8–10 in the blanks provided.

8. Some of the differences in monopolistic competitors' products are physical. What other kinds of differences might exist for products in this market?

   _____

   _____

9. Why does a monopolistic competitive firm try to differentiate its product from that of its competitors?

   _____

   _____

   _____

   _____

10. Most clothing producers are monopolistic competitors. When you go clothes shopping, what factors determine what jeans or shirts you buy? Do you see why firms try to differentiate their products?

   _____

   _____

   _____

Name: _____ Date: _____

CHAPTER 8, SECTION 4

An Oligopolistic Market

Characteristics

In questions 1–3, list the conditions of an oligopolistic market.

1. _____

_____

2. _____

_____

3. _____

_____

The characteristics of an oligopolistic market determine certain characteristics and behavior of the sellers in the market. Write your answers to questions 4–7 in the blanks provided.

4. Is an oligopolist a price taker or a price searcher?

_____

5. How do economists identify oligopolistic industries?

_____

_____

_____

_____

6. Why might oligopolistic firms be tempted to enter into a cartel agreement?

_____

_____

7. Why do cartels usually fail?

_____

_____

_____

_____

Applying the Principles Workbook   © EMC Publishing

Price Discrimination

Questions 8 and 9 concern price discrimination. Write your answers in the blanks provided.

8. Suppose you (age 17) go to the zoo with your little sister (age 5), your mother (age 42) and your grandfather (age 66). When you arrive at the zoo, you find the following sign at the admission stand.

Children (age 0-6)	$3
Students (age 6-18 with school ID)	$4
Senior Citizens (over 65)	$6
General Admission	$8

Your mother mumbles something about age discrimination under her breath. You ask what she means, and she explains that although she may enjoy the zoo the least, she is charged the most. She says, "Your little sister, who likely enjoys the zoo the most, is charged the least. What an unfair pricing system!" Having mastered your recent economics quiz on price discrimination, how would you explain the purpose of the zoo pricing structure?

_____

_____

_____

_____

_____

_____

_____

_____

9. Stores often offer mail-in rebates for some of the products they sell. How are mail-in rebates a form of price discrimination?

_____

_____

_____

_____

_____

_____

_____

Name: _____ Date: _____

CHAPTER 9, SECTION 1

What Determines Wages?

Wages In an Unskilled Labor Market

The following table shows the number of workers demanded and supplied at various wages in the unskilled labor market in H-Town. Use this table to respond to question 1.

UNSKILLED LABOR MARKET IN H-TOWN

Hourly wage	Number of workers	
	Demanded	Supplied
$2	14,000	2,000
$3	12,000	4,000
$4	10,000	6,000
$5	8,000	8,000
$6	6,000	10,000
$7	4,000	12,000
$8	2,000	14,000

1. Use the information in the table to draw the supply and demand curves for this labor market on the following grid. Use the wage rates (prices) and number of workers (quantities) demanded to plot the demand curve. Label it D_1. Use the wage rates and number of workers supplied to plot the supply curve. Label it S_1.

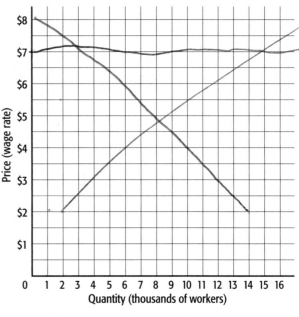

Unskilled Labor Market in H-Town

Use the graph you created in question 1 to answer questions 2 and 3.

2. The equilibrium wage for unskilled labor in H-Town is _____$5_____.

3. The equilibrium quantity for unskilled labor in H-Town is ____8,000____ workers.

Applying the Principles Workbook © EMC Publishing

Minimum Wage

Many community leaders make passionate speeches before the city council on behalf of the low-wage workers in H-Town. The community leaders maintain that the way to help low-wage workers is to raise the minimum wage. Due to the hard work and persuasive speeches, the city council of H-Town passes a law that sets the minimum wage at $7 an hour. Low-wage workers celebrate at the prospect of earning $7 an hour.

Use the above information to respond to question 4.

4. Illustrate the minimum wage by drawing a horizontal line at $7 on the graph you created in question 1.

Questions 5–10 are based on the new graph, which now shows a minimum wage of $7 an hour. Write your answers in the blanks provided.

5. The quantity demanded at the minimum wage is _____ 4,000 _____ workers.

6. The quantity supplied at the minimum wage is _____ 12,000 _____ workers.

7. The government of H-Town intended to help low-wage workers by setting the minimum wage at $7 an hour but, instead, has created a _____ surplus _____ of _____ supplied _____ workers.
   shortage   dem unled

8. Because these people are looking for work but cannot find it, they are considered _____ unemployed _____.

9. Setting the minimum wage at $7 an hour had the _____ of creating an unemployment problem in H-Town.

10. Now, suppose that many of the citizens of H-Town want to get rid of the minimum wage of $7 an hour to try to reduce unemployment. In opposition, persuasive speakers paint a picture of workers earning only $2 an hour in the absence of government regulation. Explain why this scenario is highly unlikely.

_____

_____

_____

Write your answers to questions 11 and 12 in the blanks provided.

11. Who are the winners and who are the losers when the minimum wage is increased?

_____

_____

12. Do you support an increase in the minimum wage? Why or why not?

_____

_____

Why Different Wages?

Questions 13–16 relate to the wages earned by different people. Write your answers in the blanks provided.

13. What are two of the reasons why some people earn more than others?

_____

_____

_____

14. Both doctors and sanitation workers may have a significant effect on people's health. Explain why doctors earn more than sanitation workers earn.

_____

_____

_____

15. Sally has just earned a degree in economics. She has two job offers, one from a university for $70,000 a year and one from a Wall Street investment bank for $150,000 a year. Assume Sally chooses the university job. Complete the formula that applies to this situation.

Benefits in a job =

_____

16. How much are the nonmoney benefits of the university job worth to Sally?

_____

_____

Real Wages

Real wages measure wages in terms of what the wage can buy. The formula Real wage = Money wage/CPI provides a way to compare the wages earned in different years. Questions 17–19 relate to comparing real wages.

17. Your great-grandfather, grandfather, and father are arguing about wages over dinner on Thanksgiving Day. Each claims to have had a tougher time supporting his family. Your great-grandfather earned $4,000 a year in 1940 when the CPI was 13.9; your grandfather earned $12,000 a year in 1970 when the CPI was 37.8; and your father earned $50,000 a year in 2004 when the CPI was 185.2. Rank your patriarchal line from highest to lowest according to real wages. Include the real wage value for each rounded to the nearest whole number.

Highest real wage:

_____

Second highest real wage:

_____

Lowest real wage:

_____

18. Your Aunt Judy complains that although she continues to earn more money each year, she doesn't seem to have as much buying power as she used to have. Use the real wage formula to fill in the missing numbers in the following table. Round your answers to the nearest whole number.

Year	Aunt Judy's money wage	CPI	Aunt Judy's real wage
1985	$25,000	105.5	_____
1990	$30,000	127.4	_____
1995	$35,000	150.3	_____
2000	$39,000	168.8	_____
2005	$43,000	190.7	_____

19. Is your Aunt Judy correct? Has her buying power been decreasing over time?

_____

Name: _____ Date: _____

CHAPTER 9, SECTION 2

Labor and Government Regulation

One of the objectives of a labor union may be to obtain higher wages for its members. Wages are largely determined by supply and demand in the labor market.

Write your answers to questions 1 and 2 in the blanks provided.

1. How do unions try to influence the demand for labor to achieve higher wages?

_____

_____

2. How do unions try to influence the supply of labor to achieve higher wages?

_____

_____

Each of the graphs in questions 3 and 4 shows the supply of and demand for union workers in a particular labor market. Label the axes and the demand and supply curves on the graph. Then the event described occurs. Illustrate the shift in the supply curve or the demand curve as a result of the event. Then fill in the blanks in the statements below the graph with the correct answers. (*Note:* The level of employment refers to the number of union workers employed.)

3. *Event:* The union increases demand for the good produced.

The _____ curve shifts to

the _____, the wage for

union workers _____, and

the level of employment

_____.

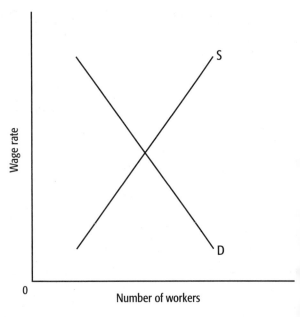

Applying the Principles Workbook © EMC Publishing

4. *Event:* The union decreases the supply of union workers.

The _____ curve shifts to the

_____, the wage for union

workers _____, and the level

of employment _____.

Write your answers to questions 5–13 in the blanks provided.

5. What is a closed shop?

_____

_____

6. What is a union shop?

_____

_____

7. Which is more restrictive, a union shop or a closed shop?

_____

8. What law made closed shops illegal?

_____

9. What is a right-to-work law?

_____

_____

10. Summarize the two major views of labor unions concerning their effects on production and efficiency.

_____

_____

_____

_____

11. Do you think labor unions are a beneficial aspect of the economy? Why or why not?

_____

_____

_____

12. The Latin phrase *caveat emptor* means "let the buyer beware." In practical terms, the phrase means that consumers are ultimately responsible for their buying decisions. Lately, government has tried to reduce the burden on consumers by regulating firms on behalf of consumers. Some people argue that the costs of regulation are too high. Other people say that consumers need the protection provided by regulation. List and discuss the costs and benefits of government regulation.

_____

_____

_____

_____

_____

13. Do you think there should be more or less government regulation? Give reasons for your answer.

_____

_____

_____

CHAPTER 10, SECTION 1

The Origins of Money

The Functions of Money

In questions 1–3, list and define the three functions of money, and then provide an example of how dollars fulfill that function. Write your answers on the lines provided.

1. *Function:*

_____

Definition:

_____

_____

Example:

_____

_____

2. *Function:*

_____

Definition:

_____

_____

Example:

_____

_____

3. *Function:*

_____

Definition:

_____

_____

Example:

_____

_____

To be used effectively as a medium of exchange, money needs to be easy to carry. And to be used effectively as a unit of account, money needs to be easily divisible into various equivalent units. For example, a dollar is easily divided into 100 equivalent units (pennies).

The items in questions 4–9 have all been used as money at one time. Analyze each item in terms of how well it functions as money, by explaining whether or not the item fulfills the functions of money. Write your answers on the lines provided.

EXAMPLE
$5 bill

Medium of exchange: <u>A $5 bill is easy to carry and functions well as a medium of exchange.</u>

Unit of account: <u>A $5 bill is easily divided into equivalent units and functions well as a unit of account.</u>

Store of value: <u>A $5 bill holds value over time and functions well as a store of value.</u>

4. large stone wheel

Medium of exchange:

_____

_____

Unit of account:

_____

_____

Store of value:

_____

_____

5. seashells

Medium of exchange:

_____

_____

Unit of account:

_____

_____

Store of value:

_____

_____

6. cattle

Medium of exchange:

_____

_____

Unit of account:

_____

_____

Store of value:

_____

_____

7. bread

Medium of exchange:

_____

_____

Unit of account:

_____

_____

Store of value:

_____

_____

8. gold

Medium of exchange:

_____

_____

Unit of account:

_____

_____

Store of value:

_____

_____

9. cigarettes

Medium of exchange:

_____

_____

Unit of account:

_____

_____

Store of value:

_____

_____

From a Barter Economy to a Money Economy

Write your answers to questions 10 and 11 on the lines provided.

10. What are the disadvantages of living in a barter economy?

_____

_____

_____

_____

_____

_____

11. How did goldsmiths increase the money supply?

_____

_____

_____

_____

_____

_____

_____

_____

_____

CHAPTER 10, SECTION 2
The Money Supply

The Components of the Money Supply

Write your answers to questions 1–5 on the lines provided.

1. The money supply can be expressed as the following equation: M1 = _____
    + _____ + _____.

2. As of August 2005, the largest part of the money supply was _____.

3. In August 2005, the money supply equaled _____.

4. Why is a nonchecking savings account considered near-money rather than money?

    _____

    _____

5. Why aren't credit cards considered money?

    _____

    _____

Borrowing, Lending, and Interest Rates

Interest rates are determined by supply and demand in the loanable funds market. Fill in the blanks in questions 6–8 with the correct answers.

6. In the loanable funds market, the demanders of loans are called _____. They are the people in the economy who wish to obtain funds in order to buy goods or services.

7. In the loanable funds market, the suppliers of loans are called _____. They are the people in the economy who have funds that they want to lend.

8. In the loanable funds market, the price is the _____. It is the price demanders must pay to obtain a loan and the price suppliers will accept to offer a loan.

In each of questions 9–12, an event has occurred that will affect demand or supply in the loanable funds market. On the graph, illustrate the shift in the supply curve or the demand curve as a result of the event. Then fill in the blanks in the statement below the graph with the correct answers.

9. The demand for loans rises.

The _____ curve shifts to

the _____ and the interest

rate _____ .

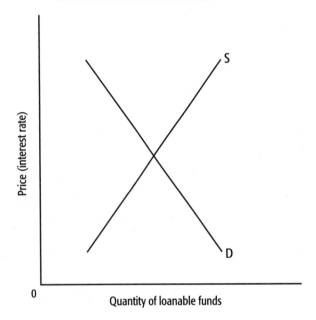

0   Quantity of loanable funds

10. The demand for loans falls.

The _____ curve shifts to

the _____ and the interest

rate _____ .

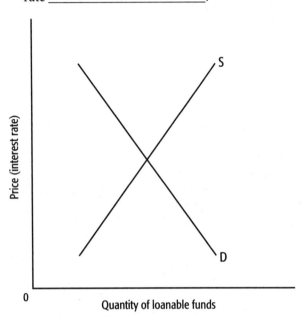

0   Quantity of loanable funds

11. The supply of loans rises.

The _____ curve shifts to

the _____ and the interest

rate _____ .

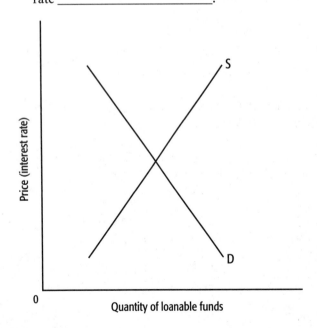

0   Quantity of loanable funds

12. The supply of loans falls.

The _____ curve shifts to

the _____ and the interest

rate _____ .

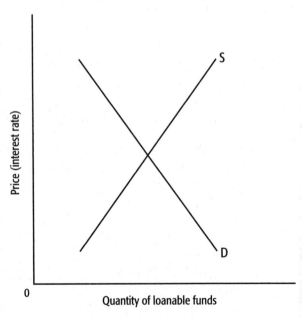

0   Quantity of loanable funds

Recall that only a change in the price of a good will change the quantity demanded or the quantity supplied of the good. Write your answers to questions 13–15 on the lines provided.

13. If the interest rate increases, what will happen in the loanable funds market?

_____

_____

14. If the interest rate decreases, what will happen in the loanable funds market?

_____

_____

15. How would you illustrate a change in the interest rate on a graph that shows supply and demand in the loanable funds market?

_____

_____

CHAPTER 10, SECTION 3

The Federal Reserve System

The Principal Components of the Fed

Write your answers to questions 1–4 on the lines provided.

1. What is the purpose of the Board of Governors of the Federal Reserve System?

_____

2. What is the structure of the Board of Governors of the Federal Reserve System?

_____

_____

3. What is the FOMC?

_____

_____

4. What is the structure of the FOMC?

_____

_____

The Major Responsibilities of the Fed

In questions 5–10, list the major responsibilities of the Fed.

5. _____

6. _____

7. _____

8. _____

9. _____

10. _____

Write your answers to questions 11–13 on the lines provided.

11. What government agency prints paper money and how does it reach the public?

_____

_____

_____

_____

12. What is a reserve account?

_____

_____

13. Suppose Olivia writes a check payable to Matt and gives it to him. What happens to the check?

_____

_____

_____

_____

_____

_____

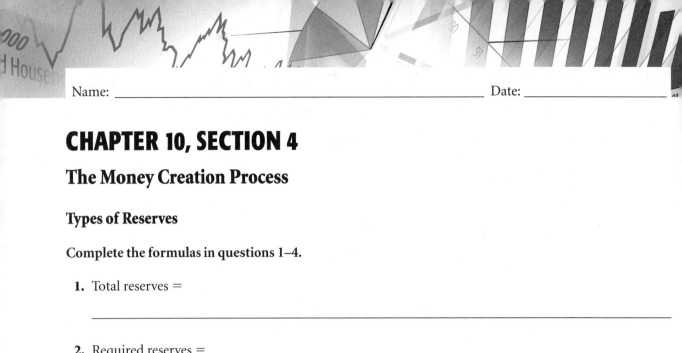

Name: _____ Date: _____

CHAPTER 10, SECTION 4

The Money Creation Process

Types of Reserves

Complete the formulas in questions 1–4.

1. Total reserves =

   _____

2. Required reserves =

   _____

3. Excess reserves =

   _____

4. Change in money supply =

   _____

How Banks Increase the Money Supply

Use the formulas from questions 1–4 to answer question 5.

5. Use the formulas to fill in the missing values in the following table. The reserve requirement is 10 percent, and all dollar amounts in the table are in millions.

	Deposits in the reserve account at the Fed	Vault cash	Checking account deposits	Total reserves	Required reserves	Excess reserves
Bank A	_____	$5	_____	$12	$1	_____
Bank B	$10	$1	$20	_____	_____	_____
Bank C	$ 3	_____	$30	_____	_____	$ 2
Bank D	$16	$4	_____	_____	$4	_____

Use the formulas from questions 1–4 and the table from question 5 to answer questions 6–10.

6. If the vault cash at bank C decreased $1 million, the excess reserves in the bank would

   _____ to _____.

7. If the Fed increased the reserve requirement to 15 percent, the required reserves in bank B would

_____ to _____ and the bank's excess reserves would

_____ to _____.

8. If the Fed decreased the reserve requirement to 5 percent, the required reserves in bank D would

_____ to _____ and the bank's excess reserves would

_____ to _____.

9. Suppose checking account deposits at bank A increased $1 million through a cash deposit by a new

account holder. Vault cash at the bank would _____ to

_____, total reserves would _____ to

_____, and excess reserves would _____ to

_____.

10. Suppose the $1 million cash deposit in question 9 magically appeared out of thin air. The money

supply would increase _____.

CHAPTER 10, SECTION 5

Fed Tools for Changing the Money Supply

Definitions of Terms

To be sure you understand some important economic terms, fill in the blanks in questions 1–3.

1. The buying and selling of government securities by the Fed is _____.

2. If a bank borrows money from the Fed, the interest rate charged by the Fed is called the

   _____.

3. If a bank borrows money from another bank rather than from the Fed, the interest rate charged by the
   second bank is called the _____.

Open Market Operations and the Discount Rate

Write your answers to questions 4–7 on the lines provided.

4. Where will a bank borrow money if the federal funds rate is greater than the discount rate? Explain.

   _____

   _____

5. Where will a bank borrow money if the federal funds rate is less than the discount rate? Explain.

   _____

   _____

6. Where does the Fed get the money to make an open market purchase?

   _____

   _____

7. What happens to the money the Fed receives from an open market sale?

   _____

   _____

Increasing or Decreasing the Money Supply

Complete the table in question 8.

8. The Fed has three tools it can use to influence the money supply. In the following table, list the three tools and then explain how the Fed uses each tool to increase or decrease the money supply.

Fed tool	To increase the money supply, the Fed	To decrease the money supply, the Fed

Name: _____   Date: _____

CHAPTER 11, SECTION 1

National Income Accounting

Determine whether or not the value of the good or service in each of the transactions in questions 1–14 is included in the calculation of this year's U.S. GDP. If the value of the good or service is not included, explain why not. Also note when the value of the good or service is included in GNP but not in GDP.

1. Mycah buys a new bicycle that was produced in Detroit.

    _____

    _____

2. Kate cashes her Social Security check.

    _____

    _____

3. John buys a used refrigerator that was produced in Cleveland.

    _____

    _____

4. Melissa buys a new Hyundai car that was produced in South Korea.

    _____

    _____

5. Bryan buys a new Hyundai car that was produced in Alabama.

    _____

    _____

6. Elizabeth, an American citizen, owns and operates a coffee shop in Mexico.

    _____

    _____

7. Don owns and operates an accounting firm in Minnesota.

    _____

    _____

8. Stacy paints her parents' house.

_____

_____

9. Goodyear sells auto tires produced in Akron to General Motors for use on new GM cars.

_____

_____

10. Dianne buys stock in Starbucks.

_____

_____

11. Travis receives cash for repairing a neighbor's lawnmower.

_____

_____

12. Bruce buys bootlegged CDs from a man on the street.

_____

_____

13. Dawn prepares a new area of her yard for a vegetable garden.

_____

_____

14. Jonah buys a new dishwasher for his house. The dishwasher was produced in Texas.

_____

_____

CHAPTER 11, SECTION 2

Measuring GDP

Economists use the equation GDP = C + I + G + EX − IM to calculate gross domestic product (GDP). In questions 1–5, state what category of spending each variable in the equation stands for and then describe what is included in each category.

1. C stands for

_____

_____

2. I stands for

_____

_____

3. G stands for

_____

_____

4. EX stands for

_____

_____

5. IM stands for

_____

_____

In questions 6–15, identify the category into which the transaction should be placed by writing C, I, G, EX, or IM in the space provided. If the value of the good or service in the transaction is not included in GDP, indicate this by writing "not GDP" in the space.

6. _____ The U.S. government spends $5 billion to improve highways.

7. _____ Todd buys a new washing machine for his home.

8. _____ Judy buys a new computer for her engineering firm.

9. _____ Pfizer sells pharmaceuticals to a company in Germany.

10. _____ Bruce buys a Honda that was made in Japan.

11. _____ General Electric spends $10 million to build a new factory in New York.

12. _____ Mei-Ling buys stock in Google.

13. _____ The U.S. government pays your grandfather $500 as part of his Social Security entitlement.

14. _____ Melissa pays her hair stylist $50 for a haircut.

15. _____ Widgets, Inc., buys new vans to update its aging fleet of delivery vehicles.

In questions 16–19, identify the spending component of GDP (C, I, G, EX, or IM) that will be affected by the event described. Then state whether GDP will rise or fall due to the event, assuming no other spending component of GDP changes.

16. Consumers choose to buy small foreign cars rather than domestic cars.

Spending component: _____   GDP will _____.

17. Business spending on factories and equipment increases.

Spending component: _____   GDP will _____.

18. Congress passes a bill that includes a large amount of money earmarked for education.

Spending component: _____   GDP will _____.

19. Consumers go on spending sprees all across the country, buying goods with the _Made in the USA_ label.

Spending component: _____   GDP will _____.

Per capita GDP is one measure of the standard of living in a country. In questions 20–22, calculate the per capita GDP rounded to the nearest dollar.

20. Country A has a population of 486,000 and a GDP of $27 billion. Per capita GDP is

_____.

21. Country B has a population of 127 million and a GDP of $3.745 trillion. Per capita GDP is

_____.

22. Country C has a population of 4.5 million and a GDP of $183 billion. Per capita GDP is

_____.

23. Complete the following table to compare the countries in questions 20–22.

	GDP	Per capita GDP
Country with highest	_____	_____
Country with second highest	_____	_____
Country with lowest	_____	_____

24. Are the people in the country that has the highest per capita GDP in question 23 better off? Explain your answer.

_____

_____

_____

CHAPTER 11, SECTION 3
Real GDP

Write your answers to questions 1 and 2 in the blanks provided.

1. Why do economists want to know real GDP?

   _____

   _____

   _____

2. Assume you live in an economy that only produces basketballs. Fill in the missing numbers in the following table. In 1987, the base year, the price of basketballs was $19.

Year	Price of basketballs	Quantity of basketballs produced	GDP	Real GDP
2000	$25	15,000	_____	_____
2001	$27	13,000	_____	_____
2002	$29	16,000	_____	_____
2003	$32	15,000	_____	_____

Use the table in question 2 to answer questions 3–7.

3. In what year was GDP highest? _____

4. In what year was real GDP highest? _____

5. What would real GDP be in 2003 if 2000 were the base year? _____

6. What is true about GDP and real GDP in the base year? Explain.

   _____

   _____

   _____

7. Suppose you didn't know the price of basketballs or the quantity produced in 2000 and 2003. Which measure provides more information about price and quantity produced in these two years, GDP or real GDP? Explain your answer.

   _____

   _____

   _____

CHAPTER 11, SECTION 4

Measuring Price Changes and the Unemployment Rate

Write your answers to questions 1 and 2 in the blanks provided.

1. What is a price index?

_____

2. What is the consumer price index (CPI)?

_____

In questions 3–5, complete the formulas that relate to price and the CPI.

3. Percentage change in price =

_____

4. $CPI_{current year}$ =

_____

5. Percentage change in CPI =

_____

The formulas in questions 3–5 are used in questions 6–20. Write your answers to questions 6–8 in the blanks provided.

6. Your favorite lunch is a hamburger and fries at the local Burger Barn. Last year, your favorite lunch was $5.95. This year, the same meal is $6.55. What was the percentage change in price?

_____

7. In 1967, the minimum wage was $1.00 an hour and the CPI was 32.9. In 1977, the minimum wage was $2.30 an hour and the CPI was 58.5. Was a minimum wage worker better off in 1967 or in 1977?

_____

_____

8. In 1985, the minimum wage was $3.35 an hour and the CPI was 105.5. In January of 2005, the minimum wage was $5.15 an hour and the CPI was 190.7. Was a minimum wage worker better off in 1985 or in January of 2005?

_____

_____

Assume the market basket includes only the goods shown in the following table. Use the table to answer questions 9–13.

Good	Quantity	Price in base year	Price in current year
Pepperoni Pizza	15	$15.00	$17.50
Bottles of Soda	30	$ 1.25	$ 1.50
DVDs	10	$17.00	$19.00

9. The total amount spent on goods in the market basket in the base year was _____.

10. The total amount spent on goods in the market basket in the current year was

   _____.

11. The CPI for the base year was _____.

12. The CPI for the current year is _____.

13. The percentage change in the CPI from the base year to the current year was

   _____.

In questions 14–18, calculate the percentage change in the CPI between the two years shown. Round your answers to the nearest tenth of a percent.

14. **Year**   **CPI**   *Percentage change in CPI:* _____
    2000   168.8
    2005   190.7

15. **Year**   **CPI**   *Percentage change in CPI:* _____
    1990   127.4
    1995   150.3

16. **Year**   **CPI**   *Percentage change in CPI:* _____
    1980   77.8
    1985   105.5

17. **Year**   **CPI**   *Percentage change in CPI:* _____
    1970   37.8
    1975   52.1

18. **Year**   **CPI**   *Percentage change in CPI:* _____
    1930   17.1
    1935   13.6

Use your answers to questions 14–18 to answer questions 19 and 20.

19. Which five-year period had the largest increase in the CPI?

   _____

20. What is unusual about the period from 1930 to 1935?

   _____

   _____

In questions 21–23, complete the formulas that relate to unemployment.

21. Civilian labor force =

_____

22. Unemployment rate =

_____

23. Employment rate =

_____

24. Use the formulas in questions 21–23 to fill in the missing numbers in the following table. Change decimal answers to percents and round to the nearest tenth of a percent.

Year	Noninstitutional adult civilian population	Employed	Unemployed	Civilian labor force	Unemployment rate	Employment rate
1990	15,000	8,178	522	_____	_____	_____
1995	15,250	8,000	_____	8,390	_____	_____
2000	15,750	_____	614	9,500	_____	_____
2005	16,000	9,400	_____	10,000	_____	_____

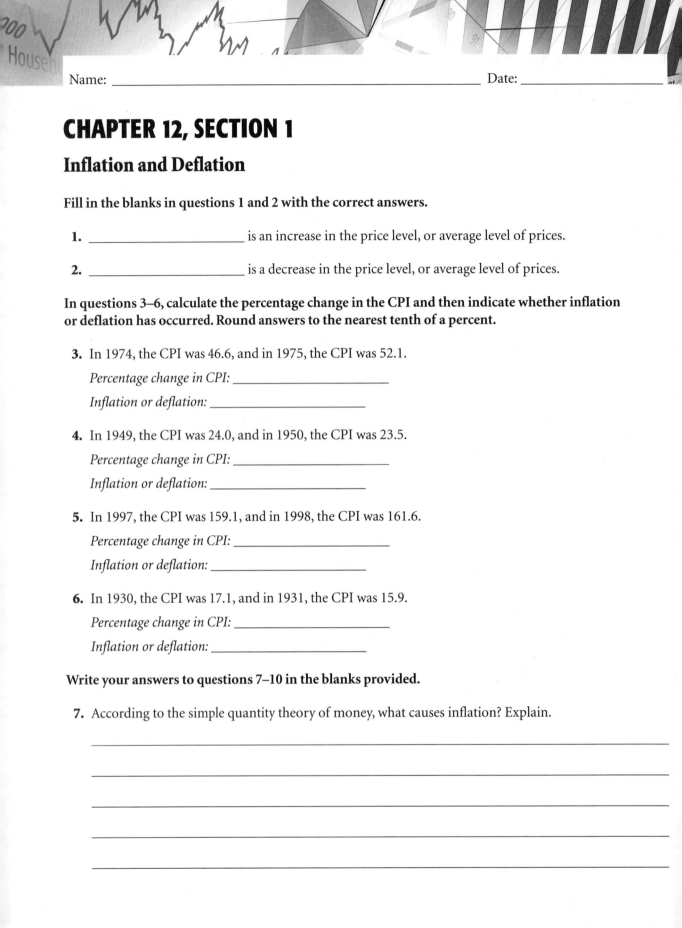

Name: _____ Date: _____

CHAPTER 12, SECTION 1

Inflation and Deflation

Fill in the blanks in questions 1 and 2 with the correct answers.

1. _____ is an increase in the price level, or average level of prices.

2. _____ is a decrease in the price level, or average level of prices.

In questions 3–6, calculate the percentage change in the CPI and then indicate whether inflation or deflation has occurred. Round answers to the nearest tenth of a percent.

3. In 1974, the CPI was 46.6, and in 1975, the CPI was 52.1.

   Percentage change in CPI: _____

   Inflation or deflation: _____

4. In 1949, the CPI was 24.0, and in 1950, the CPI was 23.5.

   Percentage change in CPI: _____

   Inflation or deflation: _____

5. In 1997, the CPI was 159.1, and in 1998, the CPI was 161.6.

   Percentage change in CPI: _____

   Inflation or deflation: _____

6. In 1930, the CPI was 17.1, and in 1931, the CPI was 15.9.

   Percentage change in CPI: _____

   Inflation or deflation: _____

Write your answers to questions 7–10 in the blanks provided.

7. According to the simple quantity theory of money, what causes inflation? Explain.

   _____

   _____

   _____

   _____

   _____

Applying the Principles Workbook   © EMC Publishing

8. At first glance, deflation would seem to be a positive occurrence for an economy. Why is deflation often destructive to an economy?

_____

_____

_____

_____

_____

9. On January 1, Jennifer puts $1,000 in a savings account that earns 4 percent interest. The inflation rate for the year is 2 percent. On December 31, will Jennifer's purchasing power have increased or decreased? Justify your answer.

_____

_____

_____

_____

_____

10. On January 1, Jerry puts $1,000 in a savings account that earns 4 percent interest. The inflation rate for the year is 6 percent. On December 31, will Jerry's purchasing power have increased or decreased? Justify your answer.

_____

_____

_____

_____

In each of questions 11–14, an event has occurred that will affect aggregate demand or aggregate supply. On the graph, illustrate the shift in the AD curve or the AS curve as a result of the event. Then fill in the blanks in the statement below the graph with the correct answers. (*Note:* Identify the inflation or deflation that occurs as demand-side or supply-side.)

11. The Fed increases the money supply.

The _____ curve shifts to the

_____, the price level

_____, and

_____ occurs.

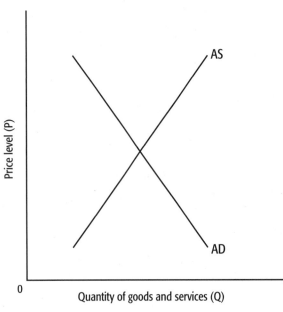

12. The Fed decreases the money supply.

The _____ curve shifts to the

_____, the price level

_____, and

_____ occurs.

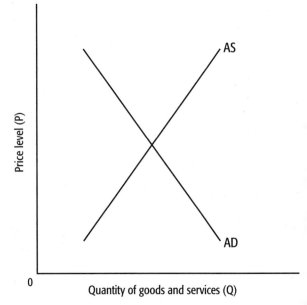

13. A drought destroys crops across the Midwest section of the United States.

The _____ curve shifts to the

_____, the price level

_____, and

_____ occurs.

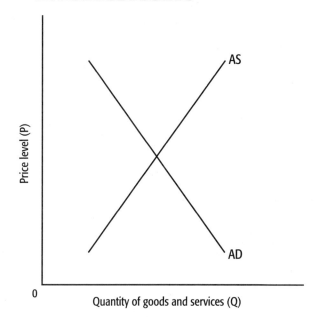

14. New technology makes it possible to produce more goods and services with existing resources.

The _____ curve shifts to the

_____, the price level

_____, and

_____ occurs.

CHAPTER 12, SECTION 2

Business Cycles

Phases

In questions 1–5, list the phases of the business cycle. Then describe what is happening to real GDP in each phase.

1. *Phase:*

_____

Description:

_____

_____

2. *Phase:*

_____

Description:

_____

_____

3. *Phase:*

_____

Description:

_____

_____

4. *Phase:*

_____

Description:

_____

_____

Applying the Principles Workbook

5. *Phase:*

_____

Description:

_____

_____

Write your answers to questions 6–10 in the blanks provided.

6. What is the difference between a recession and a depression?

_____

_____

_____

7. In which phase of the business cycle do you think the economy would be most likely to experience inflation?

_____

_____

8. In which phase of the business cycle do you think the economy would be most likely to experience high unemployment?

_____

_____

9. Which type of economic indicator would be most helpful in predicting a change in economic conditions?

_____

_____

10. What are some examples of the type of economic indicator you identified in question 9?

_____

_____

Causes

Different economists identify different causes of a business cycle. These causes may affect the expansion phase of the business cycle when real GDP is increasing, the contraction phase of the business cycle when real GDP is declining, or both the contraction and expansion phases.

Based on the above information, respond to question 11.

11. In the following table, list the causes of a business cycle that have been identified by various economists. Then describe how each cause is believed to lead to expansion or contraction.

Cause	How it leads to expansion	How it leads to contraction

Applying the Principles Workbook

CHAPTER 12, SECTION 3
Economic Growth

Write your answers to questions 1–4 in the blanks provided.

1. What is the difference between absolute real economic growth and per capita real economic growth?

   _____

   _____

   _____

2. Can real GDP increase and per capita real GDP decrease at the same time? Explain.

   _____

   _____

3. Would you rather live in a country with absolute real economic growth or in a country with per capita real economic growth? Explain.

   _____

   _____

4. How can economic growth be achieved if an economy is currently producing at a point on its PPF?

   _____

   _____

Per capita real GDP is often used as a measure of standard of living. Use the Rule of 72 to answer questions 5–8.

5. If the annual growth rate of per capita real GDP is 1 percent, your standard of living will double in _____ years.

6. If the annual growth rate of per capita real GDP is 2 percent, your standard of living will double in _____ years.

7. If the annual growth rate of per capita real GDP is 3 percent, your standard of living will double in _____ years.

8. If the annual growth rate of per capita real GDP is 4 percent, your standard of living will double in _____ years.

In questions 9–14, list the factors that can cause economic growth by inducing a rightward shift in an economy's PPF. Then explain how each factor relates to economic growth.

9. *Factor:*

_____

Explanation:

_____

_____

_____

10. *Factor:*

_____

Explanation:

_____

_____

_____

11. *Factor:*

_____

Explanation:

_____

_____

_____

12. *Factor:*

_____

Explanation:

_____

_____

_____

13. *Factor:*

_____

Explanation:

_____

_____

_____

14. *Factor:*

_____

Explanation:

_____

_____

_____

Write your answers to questions 15–17 in the blanks provided.

15. If you could rule the United States for a day, what changes would you make to ensure future economic growth?

_____

_____

_____

_____

16. An ongoing debate in society involves whether or not more (or faster) economic growth is beneficial. Summarize the views of the two sides of this debate.

_____

_____

_____

_____

_____

_____

_____

17. Which side of the debate in question 16 do you support? Why?

_____

_____

_____

_____

_____

_____

_____

CHAPTER 13, SECTION 1

Fiscal Policy

Government uses fiscal policy to achieve particular economic goals. Fill in the blanks in questions 1–6 to be sure you understand fiscal policy.

1. If government increases _____, reduces _____, or both, government is said to be implementing expansionary fiscal policy.

2. If government decreases _____, raises _____, or both, government is said to be implementing contractionary fiscal policy.

3. According to some economists, government can use expansionary fiscal policy to reduce

   _____.

4. According to some economists, government can use contractionary fiscal policy to reduce

   _____.

5. Because high unemployment is most likely to occur during the _____ phase of the business cycle, government might consider using _____ fiscal policy at this time.

6. Because high inflation is most likely to occur during the _____ phase of the business cycle, government might consider using _____ fiscal policy at this time.

7. When government implements fiscal policy, it acts to change taxes, government spending, or both. Complete the following table by explaining for each type of fiscal policy how some economists believe changing taxes or government spending affects the economy.

	Expansionary fiscal policy	Contractionary fiscal policy
Taxes		
Government spending		

Use the following key to label each of the government actions in questions 8–12 as expansionary or contractionary fiscal policy.

    E = expansionary fiscal policy
    C = contractionary fiscal policy

8. _____ The government cuts income tax rates.

9. _____ The government eliminates most tax deductions and tax credits.

10. _____ The government increases spending for education.

11. _____ The government raises the Social Security tax rate.

12. _____ The government cuts funding to the NASA program.

For each of the economic problems described in questions 13–17, determine the type of fiscal policy that might be used to solve the problem. Then indicate whether taxes and government spending should be increased or decreased to implement the fiscal policy.

13. The economy is growing at a rapid pace and the inflation rate has hit 9 percent.

Type of fiscal policy:

_____

Taxes:

_____

Government spending:

_____

14. The unemployment rate hit 11 percent last month.

Type of fiscal policy:

_____

Taxes:

_____

Government spending:

_____

15. Corporations are recording record profits and the incomes of consumers are rising rapidly; economists worry that the economy may be growing too rapidly.

Type of fiscal policy:

_____

Taxes:

_____

Government spending:

_____

16. The stock market has been declining for several weeks, and surveys show that consumer confidence is at a four-year low. Economists worry that the economy may be slowing.

Type of fiscal policy:

_____

Taxes:

_____

Government spending:

_____

17. The economy has been lagging; real GDP reports have been negative for three consecutive quarters.

Type of fiscal policy:

_____

Taxes:

_____

Government spending:

_____

Write your answers to questions 18–20 in the blanks provided.

18. How might complete crowding out make expansionary fiscal policy ineffective?

_____

_____

_____

_____

19. How might complete crowding in make contractionary fiscal policy ineffective?

_____

_____

_____

_____

20. According to supply-side economists, how can a reduction in personal income tax rates increase tax revenues?

_____

_____

_____

_____

CHAPTER 13, SECTION 2
Monetary Policy

The Federal Reserve uses monetary policy to achieve particular economic goals. Fill in the blanks in questions 1–6 to be sure you understand monetary policy.

1. If the Fed increases _____, it is said to be implementing _____ monetary policy.

2. If the Fed decreases _____, it is said to be implementing _____ monetary policy.

3. According to many economists, the Fed should use expansionary monetary policy to reduce _____.

4. According to many economists, the Fed should use contractionary monetary policy to reduce _____.

5. The Fed is most likely to use expansionary monetary policy during the _____ phase of the business cycle.

6. The Fed is most likely to use contractionary monetary policy during the _____ phase of the business cycle.

7. Recall that the Fed has three tools it can use to influence the money supply. Complete the following table by explaining how the Fed uses each tool to reduce unemployment or inflation.

Fed tool	To reduce the unemployment rate,	To reduce inflation,
Reserve requirement		
Open market operations		
Discount rate		

Some economists believe monetary policy should be implemented by using the exchange equation to achieve a stable price level. Write your answers to questions 8–12 in the blanks provided.

8. Complete the following version of the exchange equation: $\%\Delta M =$

_____

9. If the average annual change in quantity is 4 percent, the average annual change in velocity is 2 percent, and the objective is to keep prices stable, then how should the Fed change the money supply?

_____

10. If the average annual change in quantity is 7 percent, the average annual change in velocity is 3 percent, and the objective is to keep prices stable, then how should the Fed change the money supply?

_____

11. If the average annual change in quantity is 2 percent, the average annual change in velocity is 4 percent, and the objective is to keep prices stable, then how should the Fed change the money supply?

_____

12. If the average annual change in quantity is 5 percent, the average annual change in velocity is 0 percent, and the objective is to keep prices stable, then how should the Fed change the money supply?

_____

CHAPTER 13, SECTION 3

Stagflation: The Two Problems Appear Together

Fill in the blanks in questions 1–3 with the correct answers.

1. Stagflation is the occurrence of _____ and _____ at the same time.

2. If the economy is experiencing stagflation and either fiscal or monetary expansionary policy is implemented, the _____ problem is likely to be solved but the _____ problem is likely to be made worse.

3. If the economy is experiencing stagflation and either fiscal or monetary contractionary policy is implemented, the _____ problem is likely to be solved but the _____ problem is likely to be made worse.

Economists disagree about the cause of stagflation. Some believe that an erratic monetary policy causes stagflation, while others believe a marked decrease in aggregate supply can also cause stagflation. Write your answers to questions 4–7 in the blanks provided.

4. Suppose a sharp fall in the market supply of oil increases the costs of producing goods and services. As a result, aggregate supply decreases. On the following graph, illustrate the shift in the AS curve.

5. As a result of the shift of the AS curve in question 4, the price level _____ and real GDP _____.

6. An increase in the price level is _____, and a decline in real GDP leads to a rise in _____. The result of the decrease in aggregate supply is _____.

7. How might an erratic monetary policy (a stop-and-go, on-and-off monetary policy) cause stagflation?

_____

_____

_____

_____

_____

_____

_____

In the stagflation of the 1970s, Paul Volcker, chairman of the Fed at the time, attacked inflation first, which caused a further increase in unemployment. After inflation was under control, Volcker worked to reduce unemployment. Although he is given much credit in hindsight, Volcker was among the most unpopular men in America at the time because of the unemployment that resulted as his policies took effect.

Write your answers to questions 8 and 9 in the blanks provided.

8. What monetary action would Volcker have taken to attack inflation?

_____

_____

_____

9. What monetary action would Volcker have taken to reduce unemployment?

_____

_____

_____

CHAPTER 14, SECTION 1

Taxes

The amount of income taxes a person owes depends on the tax rate, the person's total income for the year, and any adjustments the person is allowed to make. A **tax deduction** is subtracted from total income *before* figuring the amount of taxes owed. A person's **taxable income** is the amount of income after these deductions are subtracted. Taxable income is multiplied by the tax rate to find the amount of taxes owed if no credits can be taken. A **tax credit** is subtracted from the amount of taxes owed *after* figuring this amount.

Assume a nation taxes the income of a single person based on the following table. Use the table to answer questions 1–7.

Taxable income	Tax rate
$0–$25,000	15%
$25,001–$50,000	25%
$50,001–$75,000	30%
$75,001–$160,000	35%
$160,001 and over	40%

1. If your taxable income for the year is $55,000, how much income tax do you owe?

   _____

2. If your total income for the year is $55,000 and you have $10,000 in tax deductions, how much income tax do you owe? _____

3. If your taxable income for the year is $55,000 and you have $1,000 in tax credits, how much income tax do you owe? _____

4. If your total income for the year is $55,000 and you have $10,000 in tax deductions and $1,000 in tax credits, how much income tax do you owe? _____

5. Is the tax structure described by the table above regressive, progressive, or proportional?

   _____

6. If a politician seeking reelection promised a tax cut for everyone, what would the politician have to cut to keep her or his promise?

   _____

   _____

7. Suppose that the nation's tax structure described on the previous page were changed to a proportional tax structure. What would the tax rate (to the nearest percent) have to be for you to pay less in income tax than the amount you paid in question 4? Justify your answer.

_____

In questions 8–10, assume that income up to and including $90,000 is subject to a Social Security tax and that income over $90,000 is not subject to the tax. Also assume the Social Security tax rate is 6 percent. Write your answers on the lines provided.

8. If your income is $150,000, how much Social Security tax do you have to pay? What percentage of you income do you pay in Social Security taxes?

_____

_____

9. If your income is $50,000, how much Social Security tax do you have to pay? What percentage of your income do you pay in Social Security taxes?

_____

_____

10. Is this Social Security tax structure regressive, progressive, or proportional? Explain.

_____

_____

CHAPTER 14, SECTION 2

The Budget: Deficits and Debt

On the circles provided in questions 1 and 2, draw pie charts that show federal government tax revenue and federal government spending. Divide the circles and label the sections using the percentages in your text. (*Note:* Each circle will have a section labeled *Other.*)

1.   **2.**

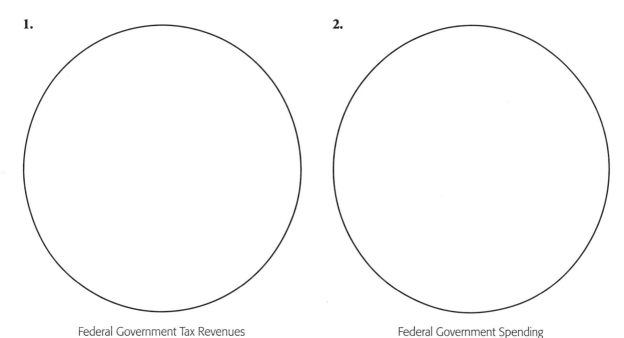

          Federal Government Tax Revenues   Federal Government Spending

Write your answers to questions 3–10 in the blanks provided.

3. The following events are not listed in the order in which they occur. Number the events in chronological order from 1 to 4.

   _____ The budget is presented to Congress.

   _____ The full Congress votes and passes the budget.

   _____ Congressional committees and subcommittees scrutinize the budget.

   _____ The president of the United States prepares the budget.

4. What is the difference between the benefits-received and the ability-to-pay principles of taxation?

   _____

   _____

   _____

   _____

   _____

5. Identify each of the following as an example of the ability-to-pay principle of taxation or an example of the benefits-received principle of taxation.

   a. The federal income tax structure is progressive. _____

   b. A state's automobile license fees finance highway maintenance. _____

6. To implement expansionary fiscal policy, the federal government can decrease taxes and/or increase spending. What effect might these actions have on the federal budget?

   _____

   _____

   _____

7. To implement contractionary fiscal policy, the federal government can increase taxes and/or decrease spending. What effect might these actions have on the federal budget?

   _____

   _____

   _____

8. What is the difference between a budget deficit and the national debt?

   _____

   _____

   _____

   _____

9. Why might your generation end up paying the debt incurred by the spending of your parents' generation?

   _____

   _____

   _____

   _____

10. Does what the government spends its revenue on matter to future generations?

   _____

   _____

   _____

   _____

CHAPTER 15, SECTION 1
International Trade

Terms

Fill in the blanks in questions 1–3 to be sure you understand some important economic terms that relate to trade.

1. When a country can produce more of a good than another country can produce with the same quantity of resources, the first country has a(n) _____ in the production of the good.

2. When a country _____ in the production of a good, it produces only that good.

3. When a country can produce a good at a lower opportunity cost than that of another country, the first country has a(n) _____ in the production of the good.

Opportunity Costs

Stacy and Travis both produce garden ornaments, including bamboo wind chimes and wooden birdhouses. Stacy and Travis make the wind chimes and birdhouses by assembling parts manufactured by other people. The following table shows the number of wind chimes and birdhouses that Stacy and Travis can make in one hour.

Use the table to answer questions 4–8.

	Wind chimes	Birdhouses
Stacy	3	1
Travis	2	3

4. When Stacy spends one hour making _____ wind chime(s), she gives up the opportunity to make _____ birdhouse(s). So for Stacy, the opportunity cost of making a wind chime is _____ birdhouse(s).

5. When Stacy spends one hour making _____ birdhouse(s), she gives up the opportunity to make _____ wind chime(s). So for Stacy, the opportunity cost of making a birdhouse is _____ wind chime(s).

6. When Travis spends one hour making _____ wind chime(s), he gives up the opportunity to make _____ birdhouse(s). So for Travis, the opportunity cost of making a wind chime is _____ birdhouse(s).

7. When Travis spends one hour making _____ birdhouse(s), he gives up the opportunity to make _____ wind chime(s). So for Travis, the opportunity cost of making a birdhouse is _____ wind chime(s).

8. Fill in the blanks to summarize Stacy's and Travis's opportunity costs for 1 wind chime (W) and 1 birdhouse (B).

Opportunity cost of 1 wind chime

Stacy: 1W = _____ B

Travis: 1W = _____ B

Opportunity cost of 1 birdhouse

Stacy: 1B = _____ W

Travis: 1B = _____ W

Comparative Advantage

Use the results you summarized in question 8 to answer questions 9–17.

9. Who has a comparative advantage in making wind chimes? Explain.

_____

_____

10. Who has a comparative advantage in making birdhouses? Explain.

_____

_____

11. Who should specialize in making wind chimes? Why?

_____

_____

12. Who should specialize in making birdhouses? Why?

_____

_____

13. If she doesn't specialize and spends one hour making wind chimes and one hour making birdhouses, Stacy makes _____ wind chime(s) and _____ birdhouse(s). If she specializes and spends both hours making wind chimes, Stacy makes _____ wind chime(s).

14. If he doesn't specialize and spends one hour making wind chimes and one hour making birdhouses, Travis makes _____ wind chime(s) and _____ birdhouse(s). If he specializes and spends both hours making birdhouses, Travis makes _____ birdhouse(s).

15. If Stacy and Travis do not specialize and each spends one hour making wind chimes and one hour making birdhouses, then together they produce _____ wind chimes and _____ birdhouses.

16. If Stacy and Travis specialize and spend two hours working in the area in which each has a comparative advantage, then together they produce _____ wind chimes and _____ birdhouses.

17. Suppose that a manufacturing firm decides to specialize in production. What might the results of such specialization be?

_____

_____

_____

_____

Advantage and Specialization

Suppose two nations, Smithville and Jonesland, can produce wheat and rice. The following table shows the combinations of the two goods that each country can produce with the same amount of resources. Write your answers to questions 18–21 on the lines provided.

Smithville
Combination A: 90 wheat and 0 rice
Combination B: 60 wheat and 10 rice
Combination C: 30 wheat and 20 rice
Combination D: 0 wheat and 30 rice

Jonesland
Combination E: 15 wheat and 0 rice
Combination F: 10 wheat and 5 rice
Combination G: 5 wheat and 10 rice
Combination H: 0 wheat and 15 rice

18. Which country has an absolute advantage in producing wheat? Why?

_____

_____

_____

19. Which country has an absolute advantage in producing rice? Why?

_____

_____

_____

20. Which country has a comparative advantage in producing wheat? Explain.

_____

_____

_____

21. Which country has a comparative advantage in producing rice? Explain.

_____

_____

_____

When the two countries do not specialize or trade, Smithville produces and consumes combination B (60 wheat and 10 rice) and Jonesland produces and consumes combination F (10 wheat and 5 rice). Now suppose Smithville and Jonesland decide to specialize in the good in which each has a comparative advantage and agree to trade 20 units of wheat for 10 units of rice.

Write your answers to questions 22–24 on the lines provided.

22. What good should each country specialize in producing and how much of the good should it produce?

_____

_____

_____

23. Complete the following to show the amount of each good each country has after specializing and trading.

Smithville: _____ wheat and _____ rice

Jonesland: _____ wheat and _____ rice

24. Complete the following to show the benefits for each country of specialization and trade.

Smithville: _____ more units of wheat and _____ more units of rice

Jonesland: _____ more units of wheat and _____ more units of rice

Outsourcing and Offshoring

Write your answers to questions 25 and 26 on the lines provided.

25. What is the difference between outsourcing and offshoring?

_____

_____

_____

26. Why might politicians speak against offshoring but not mention the benefits of offshoring?

_____

_____

_____

_____

_____

_____

_____

_____

CHAPTER 15, SECTION 2

Trade Restrictions

Tariffs and Quotas

The two major trade restrictions are tariffs and quotas. Write your answers to questions 1–7 in the blanks provided.

1. What is a tariff?

    _____

    _____

2. Who benefits from a tariff?

    _____

    _____

3. What is the effect of a tariff on consumers?

    _____

    _____

4. What is a quota?

    _____

    _____

5. Who benefits from a quota?

    _____

    _____

6. What is the effect of a quota on consumers?

    _____

    _____

7. Why is government often more responsive to producer interests than to consumer interests?

    _____

    _____

    _____

    _____

Arguments for Trade Restrictions

Arguments have been advanced for trade restrictions. For questions 8–12, list and explain the arguments in favor of trade restrictions. Then explain the criticism of each argument.

8. *Argument:*

_____

Explanation:

_____

_____

_____

Criticism:

_____

_____

_____

9. *Argument:*

_____

Explanation:

_____

_____

_____

Criticism:

_____

_____

_____

10. *Argument:*

_____

Explanation:

_____

_____

_____

Criticism:

_____

_____

_____

11. *Argument:*

_____

Explanation:

_____

_____

_____

Criticism:

_____

_____

_____

12. *Argument:*

_____

Explanation:

_____

_____

_____

Criticism:

_____

_____

_____

Organizations

In questions 13–18, identify the full name of each organization and briefly describe its function.

13. EU

_____

_____

14. NAFTA

_____

_____

15. CAFTA-DR

_____

_____

_____

16. WTO

_____

_____

17. IMF

_____

_____

_____

18. IBRD

_____

_____

_____

CHAPTER 15, SECTION 3

The Exchange Rate

To find out how much of your money you have to pay for a foreign good, you need to follow three steps:

1. Find the exchange rate.
2. Figure out how much of your money it takes to buy 1 unit of the foreign money.
3. Multiply the number of units in the price of the foreign good by your answer to step 2.

> **EXAMPLE**
> Assume that $1 = £0.87, and you want to find the dollar price of an item that costs £25.
> *Step 1:* The exchange rate is $1 = £0.87.
> *Step 2:* If $1 = £0.87, then £1 = $(1/0.87) = $1.15, rounded to the nearest cent.
> *Step 3:* The price of the item in dollars is $1.15 × 25 = $28.75.

In questions 1 and 2, assume that the exchange rate is $1 = 25 Russian rubles.

1. How many dollars (rounded to the nearest cent) will it take to buy one ruble?

_____

2. Use your answer to question 1 to complete the following table.

	Price in rubles	Price in dollars
A Volga car	419,540	_____
A McDonald's Big Mac	160	_____
A souvenir coffee mug	430	_____
A picture book of Moscow	778	_____

In questions 3 and 4, assume that the exchange rate is 1 Swiss franc = $0.80.

3. How many Swiss francs (rounded to the nearest hundredth) will it take to buy one dollar?

_____

4. Use your answer to question 3 to complete the following table.

	Price in dollars	Price in francs
A Ford Focus car	17,000.00	_____
A McDonald's Big Mac	4.50	_____
A souvenir coffee mug	11.00	_____
A picture book of New York	19.00	_____

Imagine two countries, Narnia and Gondor. The people of Narnia use Narns as currency, and the people of Gondor use Gords as currency. The following table shows the exchange rates for Narns and Gords in two years. Use the information in the table to answer questions 5–10.

Year	Exchange rate
2005	1 Narn = 20 Gords
2006	1 Narn = 25 Gords

5. One Narn buys _____ in 2005.

6. One Narn buys _____ in 2006.

7. A Narn buys _____ Gords in 2006 than in 2005, so the Narn has

   _____.

8. One Gord buys _____ in 2005.

9. One Gord buys _____ in 2006.

10. A Gord buys _____ Narns in 2006 than in 2005, so the Gord has

    _____.

In each of the situations described in questions 11–14, determine whether you would prefer for the dollar to appreciate or depreciate relative to the euro.

11. You are planning a trip to France. _____

12. You are a U.S. businessperson whose chief competitor is a German company.

    _____

13. Your factory relies on parts imported from Germany. _____

14. Your job depends on foreign tourists visiting the United States. _____

CHAPTER 15, SECTION 4

Economic Development

In questions 1–7, list the factors that some economists believe can aid growth and development and help poor countries prosper. Then briefly describe each factor.

1. *Factor:*

_____

Description:

_____

_____

_____

_____

2. *Factor:*

_____

Description:

_____

_____

_____

_____

3. *Factor:*

_____

Description:

_____

_____

_____

_____

4. *Factor:*

_____

Description:

_____

_____

_____

_____

5. *Factor:*

_____

Description:

_____

_____

_____

_____

6. *Factor:*

_____

Description:

_____

_____

_____

_____

7. *Factor:*

_____

Description:

_____

_____

_____

_____

Write your answer to question 8 on the lines provided.

8. Do international organizations exist that might be able to help less-developed countries? If so, identify these organizations and describe how they help these countries.

_____

_____

_____

_____

_____

_____

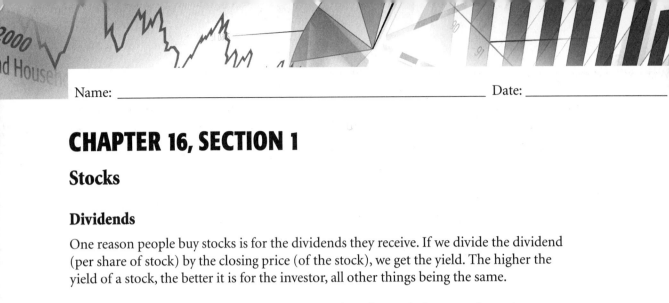

Name: _____ Date: _____

CHAPTER 16, SECTION 1

Stocks

Dividends

One reason people buy stocks is for the dividends they receive. If we divide the dividend (per share of stock) by the closing price (of the stock), we get the yield. The higher the yield of a stock, the better it is for the investor, all other things being the same.

Based on the above information and what you have learned about stocks, write your answers to questions 1–4 in the blanks provided.

1. What are dividends?

   _____

   _____

2. If you own 100 shares of company A and company A pays an annual dividend of $1.32 per share, how much would you receive in dividend payments for the year?

   _____

   _____

3. The dividend for a stock is listed as 1.43. What does this mean?

   _____

   _____

4. If the closing price of a stock is $53.48 and its dividend is $1.22, what is the yield?

   _____

Capital Gains and Losses

Another way people make money by investing in stock is by selling their stock for a price that is higher than their purchase price was. A **capital gain** is the amount of money made when stock is sold for a price that is higher than the purchase price. To calculate a capital gain, subtract the purchase price from the sale price and multiply that amount times the number of shares involved in the transactions.

Of course, stock does not always increase in value. A **capital loss** is the amount of money lost when stock is sold for a price that is lower than the purchase price. To calculate a capital loss, subtract the sale price from the purchase price and multiply that amount times the number of shares involved in the transactions.

Applying the Principles Workbook   © EMC Publishir

The entries in the following table appeared in the stock market page of a newspaper on Friday, October 14. Use the table to answer questions 5–15.

52W high	52W low	Stock	Ticker	Div	Yield %	P/E	Vol 00s	High	Low	Close	Net chg
53.17	31.93	BestBuy	BBY	0.32	0.73	20	47579	43.43	42.17	43.29	+0.79
321.28	133.40	Google	GOOG			86	84991	300.23	292.54	296.14	−1.30
46.99	41.51	Kellogg	K	1.11	2.42	20	9769	45.96	45.25	45.82	+0.23
27.94	23.82	Microsoft	MSFT	0.32	1.29	22	532632	24.73	24.48	24.67	+0.08
59.39	49.82	Pepsico	PEP	1.04	1.81	25	33994	57.85	57.18	57.51	+0.26
9.43	3.45	SiriusS	SIRI				606526	6.53	5.82	6.17	−0.25
57.89	42.33	WalMart	WMT	0.60	1.33	18	117735	45.26	44.60	45.04	+0.28

5. Which stock has the highest yield?

_____

6. If you bought 100 shares of Sirius Satellite Radio at the highest price for the year and sold it at the lowest price for the year, what was your capital loss? Explain.

_____

_____

7. If you bought 100 shares of Best Buy at the lowest price for the year and sold it at the closing price on October 14, what was your capital gain? Explain.

_____

_____

8. If you bought 100 shares of Google at the lowest price for the year and sold it at the highest price for the year, what was your capital gain? Explain.

_____

_____

9. How many shares of Microsoft traded on Friday, October 15?

_____

_____

10. What was the closing price of Pepsico on Thursday, October 13?

_____

_____

11. If you have owned 100 shares of Kellogg for a year, how much money did you receive in dividend payments last year?

_____

_____

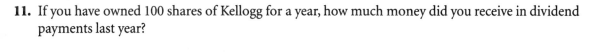

12. If you owned 200 shares of Wal-Mart, how much would you expect to receive in dividend payments this year?

_____

_____

PE Ratio

The PE ratio is obtained by dividing the closing price per share (of stock) by the net earnings per share. If a stock has a PE ratio of, say, 20, this means that the stock is selling for a share price that is 20 times its earnings per share. Write your answers to questions 13–16 in the blanks provided.

13. What might you conclude about Sirius, which has a closing price but does not have a PE ratio?

_____

_____

14. What is Wal-Mart's PE ratio and what does it mean?

_____

_____

15. What does Google's relatively high PE ratio signify?

_____

_____

_____

16. Why are people willing to buy a stock with a high PE ratio?

_____

_____

_____

CHAPTER 16, SECTION 2

Bonds

A bond is another type of investment. Write your answers to questions 1 and 2 in the blanks provided.

1. What are the three ways a company can raise money?

_____

_____

2. What is a bond?

_____

_____

In questions 3–5, list the components of a bond. Then describe each component.

3. *Component:*

_____

Description:

_____

_____

4. *Component:*

_____

Description:

_____

_____

5. *Component:*

_____

Description:

_____

_____

Elena pays $10,000 for a bond with a face value of $10,000 and a coupon rate of 6 percent. Scott buys a bond for $9,500. The face value of the bond is $10,000 and the coupon rate is 6 percent. Fill in the blanks in questions 6–14 with the correct answers.

6. Elena will receive a coupon payment of _____ each year.

7. When the bond matures, Elena will receive _____ from the issuer of the bond.

8. The yield that Elena will receive on the bond is _____.

9. If the maturity date is five years from the day Elena buys the bond, she will earn a total of

   _____ on her investment.

10. Scott will receive a coupon payment of _____ each year.

11. The yield that Scott will receive on the bond is _____.

12. When the bond matures, Scott will receive _____ from the issuer of the bond.

13. If the maturity date is five years from the day Scott buys the bond, he will earn a total of

   _____ on his investment.

14. Both Elena and Scott bought bonds with face values of $10,000, coupon rates of 6 percent, and maturity

   dates five years from the date of purchase. Scott will earn _____ on his investment

   than Elena will earn on her investment because he paid _____ than the face value

   of the bond.

Write your answers to questions 15–20 in the blanks provided.

15. What is the main difference among corporate bonds, municipal bonds, and treasury bills?

   _____

   _____

   _____

16. Which type of investment, stocks or bonds, is riskier? Why?

   _____

   _____

   _____

17. What is the relationship between the returns and the risks of various investments?

   _____

   _____

18. If a person wants high returns from investments and is willing to take high risks, he or she would likely

   invest mainly in _____.

19. If a person wants low risk investing, she or he would likely invest mainly in

_____.

20. If the yield on a 10-year Treasury bond is 4.60 percent and the yield on a 10-year corporate bond is 5.26 percent, which bond do you think would involve more risk? Why?

_____

_____

_____

CHAPTER 16, SECTION 3

Futures and Options

Futures Contracts

Different people have different tolerances for risk. Some people are willing to assume high risk and other people look for ways to insure against risk. Write your answers to questions 1–6 in the blanks provided.

1. What is a futures contract?

   _____

   _____

   _____

2. Why might Daphne, who uses a particular commodity in the production of her good, enter into a futures contract?

   _____

   _____

   _____

3. Why would Stephanie enter into a futures contract with Daphne?

   _____

   _____

   _____

   _____

4. Why might Michael, who provides a commodity, enter into a futures contract?

   _____

   _____

   _____

5. Why would Stephanie, the speculator from question 3, enter into a futures contract with Michael?

   _____

   _____

   _____

   _____

6. How can a futures contract help reduce risk?

_____

_____

Call and Put Options

Using options is a way to make money in the stock market without actually investing in stocks. It also allows a person to avoid some risk in investing. Write your answers to questions 7–13 in the blanks provided.

7. What is a call option?

_____

_____

_____

8. How does the buyer of a call option profit?

_____

_____

_____

9. What is a put option?

_____

_____

_____

10. How does the buyer of a put option profit?

_____

_____

_____

11. If you think the price of a certain stock is going to fall in the next few months, what kind of option would you buy? Why?

_____

_____

12. If you think the price of a certain stock is going to rise in the next few months, what kind of option would you buy? Why?

_____

_____

13. How could stock options as a form of compensation be used as an incentive to employees to be productive workers?

_____

_____

_____

_____

_____

_____